MW01108985

Tribute to Paula Ramsey
"Mom"

Paula Ramsey, founder & owner of "A Lady's Day Out" has gone to be with her sweet savior. On August 22, 2000 she lost her battle with cancer. Mom's life was an example for many. We can all be assured her rewards were great and that the Father welcomed her home with open arms and a big "Thank you" for a life spent glorifying Him and bringing many into the Kingdom.

"A Lady's Day Out" was Mom's vision. As with most things in her life, she was willing to share this with me. We traveled from one exciting town to the next—finding treasures and experiencing so much together for more than 10 years. I was blessed to have shared these times with my mom and hold them dear in the quiet places of my heart.

The loss of my best friend, business partner and mother is great, and the pain is deep. Our family has lost our "rock," but our faith in the Lord is strong, and we take comfort in knowing we will someday join her again in heaven.

I will miss our adventures together, but I am thankful for the times we shared, and I feel blessed to have had a mom that others could only dream of. I have always been and will continue to be proud of my mother for her love of the Lord, her right choices, her ability to lead by example and the contributions she made here on earth. Mom had an unconditional love for all of her children, and as her daughter, I will miss that attribute the most.

We will continue to publish "A Lady's Day Out" books and see her vision through. A percentage of all book sales will go to charity in Mom's memory. Thank you for celebrating her memory with us. Each time you pick up this book or any of our others, we hope you think of Mom and her inspiration—Jesus Christ.

Jennifer "Jenni" Ramsey

Fusion Art Glass
(See related story page 136.)

The Resorts of Pelican Beach
(Featured on the front cover. See related story page 50.)

Clements Antiques of Florida, Inc. *(See related story page 24.)*

Silver Shells Beach Resort and Spa
(See related stories page 42, 53 and 74.)

Madame De Elegance
(See related story page 201.)

Jackson Hill Antiques
(See related story page 190.)

Valerie Lennon, Acrylic on Canvas

Beverly McNeil Gallery
(See related story page 26.)

Bart Lindstrom, Oil on Canvas

Pied Piffle
(See related story page 162.)

Duce & Company
(See related story page 70.)

Café Provence *(See related story page 216.)*

Jean-François
Albert

McCaskill & Company
(See related story page 71.)

Capapie's Boutique
(See related story page 57.)

Paintings by Woodie
(See related story page 7.)

Quincy Art, Crafts, Toys & Games
(See related story page 142.)

Newbill Collection by the Sea
(See related story page 135.)

Seagrove Village MarketCafé
(See related story page 100.)

View from
Inn on Destin Harbor
(See related story page 37.)

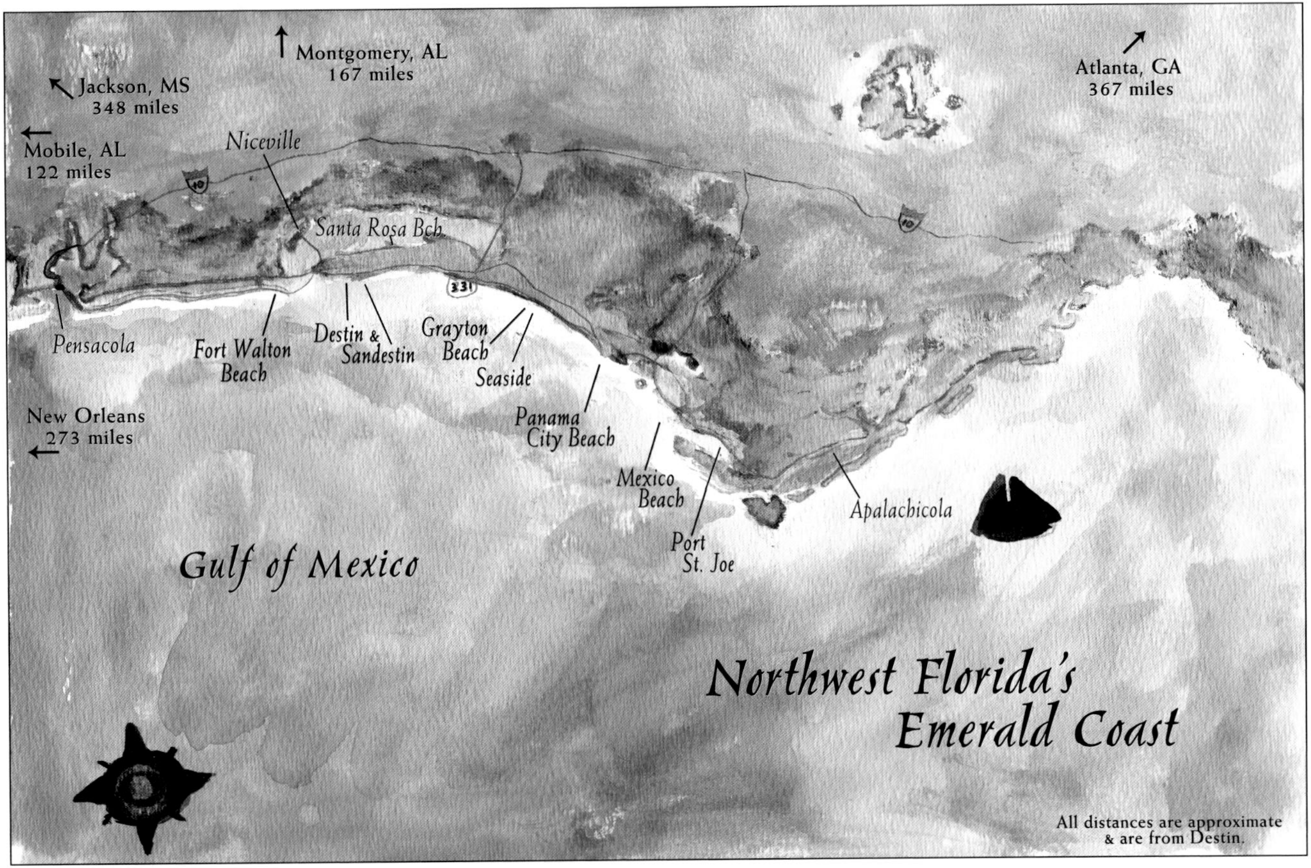

Map illustrations by: Travis Daniel DeSimone; age 13; FWB, FL.

Northwest Florida's
Emerald Coast

All distances are approximate
& are from Destin.

Atlanta, GA
367 miles

Montgomery, AL
167 miles

Jackson, MS
348 miles

Mobile, AL
122 miles

New Orleans
273 miles

Niceville

Santa Rosa Bch

Destin &
Sandestin

Grayton
Beach

Seaside

Fort Walton
Beach

Pensacola

Panama
City Beach

Mexico
Beach

Port
St. Joe

Apalachicola

Gulf of Mexico

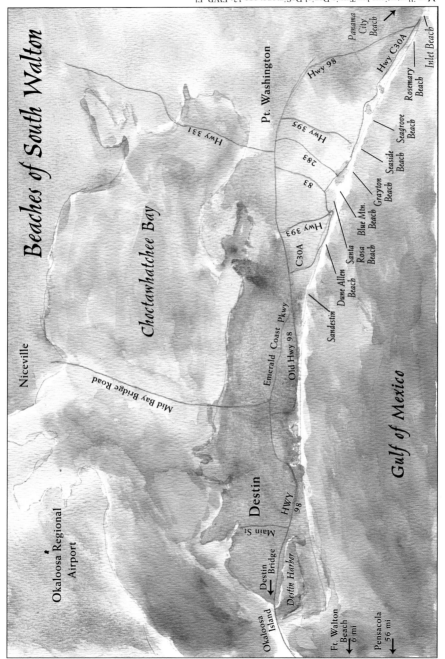

Beaches of South Walton

A Lady's Day Out
on Northwest Florida's Emerald Coast

A Shopping Guide & Tourist Handbook

— *featuring* —

Apalachicola • Carillon Beach • Destin • Fort Walton Beach
Grayton Beach • Gulf Breeze • Mexico Beach • Navarre Beach
Niceville • Pace • Panama City Beach • Pensacola
Pensacola Beach • Port St. Joe • Rosemary Beach
Sandestin • Santa Rosa Beach • Seagrove Beach
Seaside • Shalimar • Valparaiso

by Jennifer Ramsey and Peggy Adams

Cover features The Resorts of Pelican Beach
(See related story on page 50)

CREDITS

Editor/Author
Jennifer Ramsey
Peggy Adams

Director of Research & Sales
Jennifer Ramsey

Editor & Writer
Michelle Medlock Adams

Contributing Writers
Jenny Harper Nahoum
Jill Boyce
Sally Hall
Gena Maselli
Todd Winkler

Administrative & Production
Kay Payne
Beth Poulsen
Mary Manzano

Research & Sales
Peggy Adams
Nena Prejean
Tere Carter
Tina Lynch
Ashley Garrison
David Grindrod
Nancy Krenkel
Linda Lee
AnnWallace

Copyright 2003
A Lady's Day Out, Inc.
ISBN: 1-891527-14-2

Paid advertising by invitation only.

Printed in the United States of America
by Armstrong Printing Company, Austin, Texas

After enjoying this book,
we are sure you will also love our other books:

AVAILABLE TITLES

*A Lady's Day Out in the Rio Grande Valley
& South Padre Island*
A Lady's Day Out in the Texas Hill Country, Vol. II
A Lady's Day Out in Texas, Vol. II
A Lady's Day Out in Texas, Vol. III
A Lady's Day Out in Mississippi
A Lady's Day Out in Tulsa
A Kid's Day Out in the Dallas / Fort Worth Metroplex

Soon to be released:

– Spring 2004 –
*A Lady's Day Out in Nashville, Tennessee
& Surrounding Areas*

– Fall 2004 –
A Lady's Day Out in Dallas & Surrounding Areas, Vol. II

– Winter 2004 –
A Lady's Day Out in Santa Fe & Surrounding Areas

TO ORDER CALL 1-888-860-ALDO (2536)

Table of Contents

Notes from the Authors

In all of my travels, I had never spent a great deal of time exploring Florida. My impression was one of "Glitz & Glamour" with not a lot of substance—very superficial.

Well, "live and learn," as Mom used to say.

The Florida Emerald Coast, from Pensacola to Apalachicola, is a horse of a different color. I found abundant charm, excitement, peacefulness and above all—TRUE SOUTHERN HOSPITALITY. In this small section of Florida, also known as The Panhandle, I found such incredible diversity from town to town. Any vacationer will find the "PICTURE PERFECT PLACE." From fun, hip and upbeat to gentle, secluded and inspirational—the Emerald Coast has it all. I can't say enough about the Southern hospitality of the people. They are incredibly kind, welcoming and truly First Class. Oh, yeah, and they also love to have fun. If I didn't know better, I'd swear they were all from Texas!

So, go ahead. Take an extra big beach bag, full of the beach essentials. You'll come home with a beach bag full of beach treasures and memories for a lifetime.

Jennifer "Jenni" Ramsey

P.S. My favorite times were in fall and early spring. Lots of sun but not lots of crowds. Enjoy!

Dear Readers:

Remember what it was like to shop or eat out when you were growing up? Remember the places where everybody knew your name, and your parents' names, and your siblings' names, and you knew their names, too?

Hi, my name is Peggy Adams. I discovered "A Lady's Day Out," with friends while shopping in Mississippi. We were asking the cashier about a possible luncheon restaurant. She handed us a book and said, "Everything you need to know is in this book." She was right! Not only were the restaurants listed categorically by name, but also any other information you might need to know. Our restaurant choice was an extremely important decision for us— friends who had created a window of a few precious hours to be together. We were forever grateful for this fabulous little book. It had helped us immensely.

Since I adored hearing Daddy tell story after story of origins and histories, I eagerly purchased this book and fell in love with it. We drove on, and we read and read. By the time we had reached the next little town, we had planned where to eat and what to check out. Best of all, after reading some of the stories, we felt an in-depth appreciation—more of an "at home" feeling during our time spent there. It was a hint of that familiarity that I remembered from childhood.

A few weeks later I contacted Jennifer about the need for this handbook for Northwest Florida, with all its bayous and beaches. I'm very proud that A Lady's Day Out's 18th book is about our hometown and surrounding communities. We have such interesting history, wonderful shopping, and unbelievable restaurants. If you live in this area, you'll be surprised as to what you'll learn about someone you've known for years! More often than not, you will read that the motivation for different businesses grew out of the desire just to live here.

Our communities are very spread out geographically, so this guide is a fantastic trip-planning tool for tourists who come from a different state or from just the next town. It helps us understand each other. It was a gift for friends that moved Paula Ramsey, Jennifer's late mother, to write what became the first Lady's Day Out book. And, we're honored that her legacy lives on in this 18th volume. It is my wish that you, too, will feel some of that old time dimension of our area as I did in Cleveland, Miss. The stories you're about to read tell the "story behind the business" and were especially selected by a group of local friends who have lived and worked in this area for more than 20 years (see front cover). This is the book's underlying theory—to highlight selected favorites of the locals. May it help you and yours with that special "Day Out" make the most of your time together. Enjoy!

Sincerely,

Peggy Adams

P.S. I would like to dedicate this work to my sweet family, Jim, Jessica, Bo and Ashley: and to my sister in life, Judi....and to the memory of those who were living examples of giving back: T. B. (Buck) Harris; Eulalie Crawford Adams; and Teresa McAlister Adams (angels who watch over me still). In His service.

P. S. S. Call Jennifer and see if she'll write about your town.

The Evolution of the Bathing Suit

Originally called "sea bathing," swimming and visiting Florida beaches began growing in popularity with the opening of the railroad. Proper attire for beachwear at that time was known as the "bathing costume" which consisted of bloomers, black opaque stockings, a short-sleeved dress and a skirt! This bathing ensemble could be rented or purchased. All "ladies" were expected to know the specifications of skirt length as well as the allowed plunge of the neckline. Censors, armed with measuring tapes, were known to patrol the popular beaches and boardwalks keeping proper modesty in check.

Prior to the opening of the railroad, a lady's expected attire went literally from head-to-toe. Generally the style was a high-necked, stiff cotton blouse, a heavy long woolen skirt and matching jacket, a hat and, many times, a parasol.

Annette Kellerman, the first American woman swimming star, came up with an idea for something less constrictive in the water—a swimsuit! Her creative design was a loose, one-piece wool suit, which was deemed appropriate by 1910. Models and starlets on arcade-cards, in magazines, and in movies, added to people's acceptance of such a dramatic change in fashion.

The "bathing beauty" hit the big screen in 1911, with *The Diving Girl*, a Mack Sennett silent Keystone Comedy. Ms. Kellerman's innovation had paved the way for such great stars as Gloria Swanson and Esther Williams. Just after World War I, swimming suit fashion began a rapid evolution. Always a fashion leader, France designed the *clinging*, one-piece suit. Sometime around 1935, the two-piece came off the drawing board. And in 1947, came the most exciting change of all—the bikini. And today, well, almost anything goes! Long gone are the days of censors patrolling the beaches with their measuring tapes. You'll see lots of skin on today's beaches. We at A Lady's Day Out are excited about another fashion invention—the cover up!

THE INCREDIBLE
EMERALD COAST

Named for the beauty of its sparkling, clear, emerald green waters along miles and miles of pristine sugar-white sand beaches, the Emerald Coast is breathtaking! The beautiful beaches and sun-kissed skies give this part of Northwest Florida a timeless allure and ageless appeal to families seeking the perfect vacation. The unrivaled splendor of the Emerald Coast beaches, picture perfect sunrises and sunsets, spirited celebrations, incredible golf courses, and delicious seafood draw millions of visitors to this vacation paradise each year. In fact, *Southern Living Magazine* has named the Emerald Coast one of the top five "Favorite Family Vacation Destinations" for six consecutive years.

From Pensacola to Apalachicola, you'll find secret places and treasures waiting just for you. The area's unique culture and natural beauty offer visitors something out of the ordinary and wonderful. All along the gorgeous Gulf you will find a stretch of beaches, beachside restaurants, surf shops and great accommodations. Gulf bays, rivers, bayous, and nature parks abound with exciting opportunities. Your question will be, "What do I want to do first?"

If the unfettered and unhurried vacation is what you've dreamed about all year, "Florida's Forgotten Coast" or "Old Florida," will meet every expectation with its secluded beaches and privacy—beginning with the Beaches of South Walton, heading east through Mexico Beach and Port St. Joe, ending at Apalachicola. Even on the busiest weekends, you can go for long walks along almost deserted shores. Some of the small beach towns might have only one traffic light and a combination grocery store and bait shop, while others have developed into thriving artist colonies and shopping meccas. These secluded, tucked-away beaches offer a quiet retreat from the busy world. You'll see wooden railings winding downhill through the sea-oat colored dunes to the shoreline, and maybe a lone fishing pole stuck in the sand. Pelicans swirl and dive for their dinner, and almost ghostlike sand crabs scurry across the white sand.

Larger coastal cities like Pensacola, Fort Walton Beach and Panama City Beach, open up entirely different opportunities for families who want to play in the sun. The entertainment is varied and exciting, and the adventures can be fast paced and challenging. In Pensacola you can take a break from the sun and visit the Navy personnel and fighter planes at the Pensacola Naval Complex, and the National Museum of Naval Aviation, home of the famous "Blue Angles." If you've ever wondered what it is like to fly, be brave and step into the motion-based flight simulator, which simulates the feeling of flight on a carrier-based strike mission! Or grab the Safari Line Train through the zoo to see more than 700 exotic animals. Pensacola's moderate year-round temperature is conducive to outdoor activities like biking, canoeing, tubing, hunting, tennis and of course, golf. Many beautiful golf courses host tournaments throughout the year, one of the most exciting being the Senior PGA Tour Emerald Coast Classic, which draws some of the biggest names in golf.

Throughout the Emerald Coast, you'll be stunned by the beauty of its main attraction—the beaches and one of the most beautiful and most popular is Panama City Beach. It has won numerous awards for its legendary pure white sands, clear blue-green waters, dancing dolphin shows, and fiery romantic appeal. Panama City Beach has long been referred to as the "Miracle Strip" which includes rides, games, and lots of fast and furious fun. Roller coasters, ferris wheels, and candy apples will delight the "kid" in everyone, or you can plan a swashbuckling adventure aboard an authentic "pirate ship." Seaplanes, helicopter rides, and airboat adventures will take you up, up, and away for the day, but the beautiful gulf and bay waters offer visitors the most wonderful treat of all—world-class fishing. Spanish mackerel and blue fish can be found in the bays, pompano and cobia run the beaches, while the larger trophy fish can be found farther out in the Gulf. There are more than ten fishing tournaments held each year, with the most popular being the Bay Point Invitational Billfish Tournament in July. A record-setting, history-making 1,046-pound marlin weighed in during the 2001 tournament as the 14th largest in the world. Unique dive sites off the sparkling Panama City Beach waters include historical and artificial reefs, and many historic wrecked ships. In fact, the numerous wrecks available for divers to explore have given the city the title, "wreck capital of the South."

Destin/Sandestin and their surrounding communities are most likely the number one tourist destination, offering incredible shopping and dining, world-class fishing and diving, and some of the world's best golf courses. The largest fishing fleet in the state of Florida is located in Destin, which is called the "World's Luckiest Fishing Village!" Deep-sea bottom fishing is one of the specialties of Destin's fleet, hauling in red snapper, grouper, triggerfish, and amberjack. More than 100 charter and party boats are available almost year-round to ensure great success and satisfaction. Of course, as throughout all of the Emerald Coast, the beaches of Destin are legendary. Their breathtaking scenery, soothing waters and warm breezes offer experiences unrivaled anywhere else.

The Emerald Coast is a magical place. Whether you want to "treasure hunt" in the quaint shops, lie back in a beach chair with a good book and soak up the Southern charm, or enjoy a day golfing, this Florida playground has something for everyone. You might take a glass-bottom boat trip to watch the activity in the crystal water beneath you, actually swim with the dolphins in the surf, or cut through the colored waters and salty breeze in a catamaran. Enjoy shopping, watersports, fishing, hiking, horseback riding, boating, sailing, swimming, dining, golf and tennis to your heart's delight, then kick back and enjoy the show of the brilliant sunset over the water at day's end. Fine dining can be found everywhere—from the most expensive and exclusive restaurants and open-air cafés to the thatched roof huts and rickety oyster bars on the beach. The Gulf waters yield more than 20 varieties of tasty fish during a season, and the locals sure know how to cook em up!

SPECIAL PEOPLE

Just to let you know that you're in "good company" while visiting Florida, let us "drop a few names" of interesting, famous, and favorite Floridians you'll hear about during your visit.

Wayne Rogers

You'll remember him from the long-running comedy series, M.A.S.H. as Capt. "Trapper John" McIntyre. Today, Wayne Rogers spends a lot of his time on the beaches and golf courses of the Emerald Coast. He is known throughout Florida for his financial and entrepreneurial savvy in the entertainment industry.

Chris Judd

A young dancer named Chris Judd from Niceville, Fla. exploded into the Hollywood scene when he started touring with Michael Jackson on his Dangerous and History World Tours. His choreography team recently worked with Jennifer Lopez on the videos "Ain't It Funny" and "I'm Real." He has performed on the Billboard Awards with Celine Dion, the MTV Music Awards with "NSYNC," and the American Music Awards with Enrique Iglesias and Bryan McKnight.

Clint Daniels

Florida calls him "The Future of Country Music." Clint Daniels, who was born and raised in the Florida Panhandle, can remember sitting on his grandpa's knee at the age of five, when he got his first fiddle. His father plucked and sang at country music and bluegrass festivals in the hill country of Northwest Florida, and it was during these early years that it all became "second nature" to Daniels. It has been said of his talent, "He has a really pretty voice that sounds like a Mack truck coming at you. He is the future of country music." From his first "gig" in a converted gas station in Two Egg, Fla., Clint Daniels is now a bright new star in the world of country music.

Danny Wuerffel

In the wide, wide, world of sports, every armchair quarterback will recognize the name Danny Wuerffel as one of the most impressive All-American Players. Danny was a Heisman Trophy winner, a record breaker for the University of Florida, and played for the New Orleans Saints. This outstanding young man is a well-known athlete who continues to credit his relationship with God for the incredible success he has experienced in his life.

Emmitt Smith

One of Pensacola's most famous people is someone every young man would love to be—#22, Emmitt Smith. Emmitt currently holds the titles for All-time NFL Rushing Yards and All-time NFL Rushing Touch Downs.

Dick Covey

In the world of aviation, Florida is proud to list Fort Walton Beach as the home of Astronaut Richard (Dick) Covey. He graduated from Choctawhatchee High School in Shalimar, Fla. and from Purdue University in 1969. He has flown three space flights and has served as Mission Control spacecraft communicator.

Roy Jones, Jr.

Even though he barely missed the Gold Medal, Roy was voted Outstanding Boxer of the Summer Olympic Games, 1988. Today he clutches the World Boxing Association Heavyweight title belt.

Jerry Pate

He and his wife Soozi call Pensacola home now, but the world has hosted him in too many golf tournaments to name. He won the U. S. Open and Canadian Open in1976, the Phoenix Open in 1977, and the list goes on and on. Jerry has served as a color analyst on CBS, ABC, and BBC golf broadcasts during the 1990s and is involved in the golf design business. His trademark—Jerry always marks his ball with the "tails" side of a coin!

Edwin Watts

Edwin Watts and his brother Ronnie entered the golf retail business in 1968, with a small Fort Walton Beach Municipal Golf Course. Today the name is synonymous with top-quality golf equipment in more than 48 retail outlets located throughout the Southern and Eastern United States.

Dread Clampitt

Locals Balder W. P. Saunders, Kyle J. Ogle, Justin Lewis Price-Rees, and Duke Bardwell are Dread Clampitt. Have you ever heard of roots music? Keep your eyes and ears open for Dread Clampitt. This reggae-bluegrass fusion band named after Jed Clampett of the *Beverly Hillbillies* is a local favorite gone big. People ask, "What is that music? It isn't bluegrass, country, jazz, blues, heavy metal, Top-40, or pipi-tease disco. How about rock-and-roll? Is it traditional or alternative?" Best way to answer is—go, hear them, and decide for yourself. When not touring, they can be found performing in "hot spots" along the Emerald Coast. To learn more visit www.dreadclampitt.com.

What a fun and interesting place, the fascinating Emerald Coast. The beauty of the dazzling waters and pristine shores is matched only by the charming hospitality of the people here. From the moment you arrive you will feel the warmth and genuine welcome in their slow Southern voices, and relish in the fact that they love families. From tiny tots, to those of us who are still only kids at heart, everyone feels as through they are being wrapped in a soft Southern embrace (like a big fluffy towel after an ocean swim)! Families are catered to and enjoyed by the locals, and that's one reason so many people who visit, end up calling the Emerald Coast "home."

"JEWELS OF THE EMERALD COAST–THE PEOPLE"

WOODROW WILSON LONG
(WOODIE LONG)
ONE OF FLORIDA'S FAVORITE SONS

As the son of a migrant farm worker, Woodie Long learned at the tender age of three-years-old that life was hard work. He worked alongside the rest of his nine brothers and sisters as they traveled constantly "to where the work was." His job at three-years-old—to carry water to the seedlings in the fields. When he was only 14 years old, his father abandoned the struggling family, forcing Woodie to become completely independent at a very early age. He became a house painter, and like his father, moved from place-to-place "where the work was." Sometimes, he would paint lively scenes on the walls of the houses before having to paint over them. His desire to preserve his memories for his children burst forth onto paper and canvas in 1988, when he picked up his wife's brushes to create the first of many colorful, inspirational paintings.

Today, Woodie Long's folk art "memories" hang in major private and corporate collections throughout the world, but he is most proud of a piece in the Fenimore Art Museum in Cooperstown, N.Y., a leader in the "world of folk art collections." Woodie's work also graces the walls of several other museums around the country. Florida, however, is most proud of Paintings By Woodie, formerly known as Gallery of Folk Art—the little gallery tucked far into the backroads of Santa Rosa Beach. Follow the signs that say, "Woodie's Folk Art," to the simple, small cabin that is home to this incredible master artist. Woodie and his wife Dot live the most simple of lives, and are the sweetest, most sincere people you will ever meet. It's as if the magnitude of his fame has not even touched their lives. He is famous, known in all of the art circles of the United States, yet he is humble and approachable, and fiercely loved by all. Woodie captures life's experiences in paintings with titles like *Wash Day*, *Summer*, *Baptism*, *Sharecroppers on a Sunday Afternoon*, *First and Second Cousins*, and *Jumpin on Grandma's Bed*, in vibrant mesmerizing colors and textures. All are poignant creations of his sweet and sometimes bittersweet experiences as a sharecropper's son, and the scenes tug at your heart with a combination of recognition and wonder. One of the most touching scenes Woodie paints reveals not only the inspiration for the work, but an insight into the soul of this man who never knew the joy of really being "a little boy." In his painting titled "*School Bus*," Woodie paints a picture of a bright, vivid yellow school bus he watched every day as a child. He would watch it come and go each morning and afternoon, carrying happy, boisterous children to school and back while he worked the fields. His experiences on the "school bus" were limited through the years, but vivid enough to become a treasured memory he wanted to preserve on canvas. All of his paintings are as beautiful, and telling. From jazz musicians to preachers to clotheslines and swimming holds, Woodie has painted the most important people in his life, and the events that shaped his history, and the South.

You will love getting to know this quiet-spoken gentleman with the soulful eyes, warm smile, and beach-white hair as you explore the passion with which he depicts the memories of his childhood. His paintings are simplistic, yet stimulating; calming; yet exhilarating; and they are as beautiful as the South itself. You will see "his South" in his paintings, and recognize the easy way of life that people here still experience today. From every bright and beautiful color under the Florida sun to the notes of a jazz band you can almost hear, Woodie Long offers a delicious slice of life in the South in each painting. His work can be found in art galleries throughout Florida, but if you are anywhere near Santa Rosa Beach, stop by Paintings by Woodie. Don't miss the opportunity to meet this extremely talented and beautiful man and his wife who will welcome you as they would a long-time friend. Call 850-231-9961 or e-mail Woodie and Dot at dotlong@web30.com online.

BEVERLY McNEIL

With an elegance that matches the beauty of her remarkable art galleries, Beverly McNeil moves through the areas of her life with an endearing Southern gentleness. She has been involved in the world of art for more than 20 years, and is one of the most recognized art dealers in the nation. As the owner of Portrait Brokers of America, Beverly represents more than 100 of the finest painters in the United States, and has been collecting antique paintings for many years.

This beautiful, energetic mother of five, and grandmother of four, is extremely active in everything that touches their lives. One of the things she is most proud of and committed to is Community Bible Study (CBS), which she helped start a few years ago in Destin. Today, as many as 400 members meet each week to study the Bible and share with each other about God's wonderful work in their lives. She is also on the boards of the Mattie Kelly Arts Foundation, the Vanguard Bank, and CAC—Child Advocate Center.

Beverly and husband John McNeil have been dedicated to the growth and preservation of Destin and are partners in the beautiful development called Kelly Plantation. Destin matriarch, Mattie Kelly was excited about the visionary plan that would transform her former turpentine farm into what they called, "God's Masterpiece on the Bay."

Because of Beverly's long-time interest and love of fine art, she was very excited when a terrific building became available on the Emerald Coast Parkway. She knew that it would be the ideal place to locate her gallery, which has grown into one of the most beautiful businesses in the South. The Beverly McNeil Gallery has three main areas of focus, with a common goal of representing the highest quality of art and portraiture possible. The first area includes original works of art in oil, pastel, watercolor, and sculpture by some of the leading artists in the country. The second area encompasses 19th century antique English paintings and portraits, and the third area covers commissioned portraits through Portrait Brokers of America.

"Our goal is to exceed your expectations and to guarantee your satisfaction," states Beverly. Everything about the gallery will indeed "exceed your expectations." It is a beautiful place, one that invites visitors to browse leisurely, to sit and absorb the feeling of the paintings, and to enjoy a profusion of different styles and techniques of art. The diverse inventory of artwork showcases a wide range of periods and styles at all levels of market value. Beverly travels to England several times a year in search of the best sources for antique paintings and portraits. Some of these date back to the early 1800s—exquisite landscapes, figures, and animals, all in gorgeous antique frames.

Beverly McNeil has been such an inspirational force in the world of art in her beloved Destin community, and in the lives of her friends and family who watch her work tirelessly for the things she loves. Her God-given talent and obedient spirit to God's leadership throughout the years has resulted in a life that continues to be a blessing to everyone she meets. We know you will love getting to know this very "special lady!"

LINDA EYER

While gently sifting through her father's personal effects after his long, 106-year life, Linda Eyer found a beautiful picture of her mother. It was a picture she had always loved, and one that she would use as inspiration in fulfilling her dreams. The picture was of her mother, Wilhelmina, a strong, levelheaded, good businesswoman who Linda says "always ran a tight ship." Linda felt her mother's influence reaching out through the photograph and the idea for her beautiful shop formulated in that seed. She and her sister Shirley Sahlie opened the beautiful gift shop and interiors boutique called Wilhelmina. Shirley had just lost her wonderful husband of forty years, and Shirley stayed with Wilhelmina for four years, and their collective spirit still drives the business today. Linda says, "Wilhelmina was a gift of love from mother to the both of us—from me to Shirley, and then from Shirley to me. God has blessed us so richly."

She had always loved "old things," things that carried a history, things that had been loved by other people through the years. Linda says that old things give an instant comfort, warmth, friendliness, and sense of "being home." She admits that she was almost manic about collecting and refurbishing. She furnished her own home, and those of friends with exquisite collections of antiques and treasures from around the world.

Part of Linda's fascination with unusual and historical collections evolved through her many travels. She has lived all around the world—Tunisia, Saudi Arabia, Belgium, Bahrain, and Kuwait, and traveled to many other exotic places. In each of these, she recognized a similar thread that ran through the cultures of the area—people love family, tradition, and history. They love being able to preserve for the future things that were beautiful and important to them, treasures that would in some way bond the generations through the ages.

In Wilhelmina, Linda shares the stories of the past and present, with things that are old and new. She has mixed nostalgia, history, and of course wonderful Southern hospitality. Her love for the South, in particular this charming place called Grayton Beach, has greatly influenced her life through the years. Linda's family has been a part of Grayton Beach history for more than 100 years, and it was here that she brought her children every summer during those 30 years of traveling abroad. She wanted them to experience the same sense of home and tradition that she had learned during her young days here. She still says that Grayton Beach is America's heartland—blessed by God.

Coupled with her life-long love of family and tradition, it was inevitable that her future would include the Grayton Beach store called "Wilhelmina."

Thank you Linda Eyer, for holding to beautiful traditions, to the memory of those before us, and for reminding us through the beautiful collections in Wilhelmina, that sometimes it is wonderful to be somewhere between yesterday and today, (especially if you can spend it on the Emerald Coast)!

SANDRA CLEMENTS

An engaging woman with a contagious smile and effervescent personality, Sandra Clements loves family, tradition, antiques and the Emerald Coast...and you will love her! An antique auctioneer, Sandra is the owner of Clements Antiques in Destin, Fla.

As one of five children of Wallace and Doris Clements, she grew up surrounded by antiques. As a child, she worked in the family's antique business. She lived with antiques, traveled with antiques and vacationed with antiques. As her parents sought out antiques, Sandra worked alongside them, wrapping the crystal and china and packing the truck. She developed an eye for value and authenticity even at an early age.

Sandra's father, Wallace Clements, an auctioneer and pioneer in the antique business, was the first to bring an entire container of English antiques to the United States. While he conducted auctions, Sandra and the rest of her family participated. Her mother clerked while Sandra "worked the floor," watching for bids, and her sister Brenda cashiered. Sandra has wonderful memories of her childhood spent among the beautiful collections of antiques and the people who loved them.

Later, while attending the University of Tennessee, Sandra studied art history and interior design. Though she appreciated her schooling, she admits that most of her knowledge and wisdom came from her parents.

In fact, it was with the support of family and friends that Sandra began her own career as an auctioneer. Though they provided the foundation, it was Sandra's warmth, sincerity, spontaneity and considerable wit that made her a success through the years. In fact, Sandra was one of the few women appointed to the Board of Auctioneers by both Democratic and Republican governors for 10 years.

Finally in 1989, Sandra realized her dream of owning and operating her own antique shop. Walking through Clements Antiques feels like a journey through her life. Her knowledge and love of fine antiques is evident in every area of the store. In room-like settings, she arranges American, English, and French antiques from the 17th through 20th centuries. Drawing from her experiences and travels of the United States, Sandra collects exquisite period pieces like mirrors, clocks, oil paintings, porcelain, silver and cut glass. She also offers quality collectibles, such as handmade oriental rugs and Baccarat, Lalique and Waterford crystal.

Clements Antiques is an Emerald Coast treasure. It is the culmination of Sandra Clements' lifelong pursuit to embrace the art of antiquing and the excitement of passing on antiques to others. When you stop by, you'll discover her incredible knowledge about antiques and decorating, and you'll experience her energy and passion for life.

CHARLES MORGAN

Charles Morgan is truly one of Florida's most inspirational and influential natives, one Destin is extremely proud to call its own. He is the owner of one of Destin's most popular and successful restaurants. The City of Destin's Morgan Sports Complex was named in honor of the contributions Charles' family has made to Destin. He sponsors the Annual Habitat for Humanity Thanksgiving Dinner at Harbor Docks and all donations go to Habitat for Humanity. He also sponsors the annual Take-A-Kid Fishing Day, but perhaps he is best known for owning and operating Rally for Recreation/Harbor Docks Charities.

In 1979, Harbor Docks Restaurant was a little weather-beaten cottage with six picnic tables and one bathroom. At that time, it's claim-to-fame was an ancient dog named Raspberry, who lay out on the porch all day, thumping his tail at the folks who wandered up for a beer or oysters on the half shell. Things certainly have changed. Sadly, Raspberry has gone on to his reward, but the picnic tables are still there. Through the years, Morgan has "spiffed up" the restaurant with air conditioning, a paved parking lot and a few more tables. He has even added a sushi bar, a hibachi grill and a deck that sprawls along the waterfront. Harbor Docks is still a long way from "fancy," but Charles likes it that way. It is a true taste of the best of Destin.

As Morgan continued to improve Harbor Docks through the years, he noticed a need for recreation for area residents and visitors. The idea for the "Harbor Docks Rally for Recreation" was conceived and with community backing and support, it soon became a reality. Over the years, the dollar number continued to rise as, one after another, local, non-profit organizations benefited from the generous proceeds and hard work of Rally for Recreation. The money has gone to help the YMCA; to provide a 400-meter running track for the elementary school; to purchase computers and books for the new children's wing in the city library; and to support organizations like the Destin Little League. From its humble beginnings in 1986, the Rally for Recreation has raised more than $700,000. Though still under the direction of Charles Morgan, it was reorganized as Harbor Docks Charities in 2003.

An instrumental force behind each event, Charles Morgan admits that one of his favorite events is the "Take-A-Kid-Fishing-Day," which is held the first Sunday in November. A fleet of nearly 50 of Destin's finest fishing boats takes nearly 500 kids, who might normally never get the chance to experience such a fun activity, fishing for the day. They have the opportunity to learn to use a rod and reel, enjoy a meal and win prizes.

This year, as in years past, Harbor Docks Restaurant will be the site for the annual Habitat for Humanity Thanksgiving Dinner. Hundreds of people enjoy a traditional, home-style holiday feast and all donations go to Habitat for Humanity.

Charles Morgan continues to give back to the community he loves so much, acknowledging that he receives much more in return. His desire to help others less fortunate and his never-tiring enthusiasm for community growth and development will continue to benefit Destin for generations to come. He is one of the "Special People" you won't want to miss meeting during your visit to the Emerald Coast!

DISCOVER
DESTIN / SANDESTIN

There you are, walking along the sandy white beach. The sand is squishing between your toes. It feels good. You stop and watch the dolphins dancing on the emerald green waves. As the ocean breeze gently blows your hair, you watch one of the most spectacular sunsets you've ever seen. Then...the alarm goes off.

You were dreaming of Destin again, weren't you?

Well, quit dreaming, pack your bags, and head for the divine Destin and Sandestin area. It's beckoning you to experience its beautiful beaches, quality cuisine, fabulous fishing, gorgeous golf courses, awesome attractions, and stupendous shopping.

Just make sure you plan to stay awhile because there's an awful lot to see and do in these Upper Gulf Coast sea towns. The area is beautiful and mysterious while brimming in class and history.

For instance, you won't want to miss Henderson Beach State Park, named for the landowners who sold it to the state in 1983. It was the very first purchase in the "Save Our Coast Program." The Hendersons wanted some of the natural beauty preserved, so that's what the state did. Today, you'll find 6,000 feet of awesome beach; 250 acres in all; a boardwalk; bathhouses; picnic pavilions and more!

DESTIN

In the Beginning

From turpentine to tourists—Destin has quite an interesting past.

In the mid 1930s, Coleman and Mattie Kelly left their home in Washington County, Fla., for the laidback community of Destin.

Their reason for moving to the fishing village on the Gulf Coast? To farm.

They weren't concerned that farming on sandy acres wouldn't grow much of anything, because they planned to produce turpentine. During this time, "fishing families" made up the bulk of Destin's population, and the Kellys' 900-acre turpentine farm produced Destin's first significant payroll. In fact, according to an article written by Carolyn Deariso that appeared in *Emerald Coast Magazine* (Spring 2001), the Kellys' turpentine farm fueled the local economy for more than 40 years.

This entrepreneurial couple built the first cottages for tourists and launched the very first deep-sea sport fishing boat in Northwest Fla.—the Martha-Gene. Business venture after business venture flourished under the Kellys' control. People who knew the Kellys agree that the only thing that outshined their business smarts was their love for the community of Destin.

While the need for the turpentine farm dwindled over the years, the Kellys' love for Destin didn't. Coleman longed for the 900 acres to be used for something important, something meaningful. After his death in 1973, Mattie vowed to find a way to turn the turpentine farm into something special. That happened 20 years later with the emergence of Kelly Plantation. The plans were simply this: to enhance the beauty of the land rather than intrude on God's creation. Mattie was involved with every stage of planning until her death in 1992. Today, this little piece of heaven on earth is a 250-acre residential country club development with approximately half of the land designated for nature preserves, pedestrian trails, neighborhood parks, nature trails, walks, lakes and an 18-hole Fred Couples signature golf course. The area churns with friendliness and a sense of family—just like Mattie and Coleman would have wanted it.

A Little Culture, Anyone?

From the mid-1930s until Mattie's death in 1992, she was an integral part of Destin's cultural side, too. Both publicly and privately, Mattie and Coleman supported the arts, education and church growth throughout Destin. She was a gifted poet and piano player, as well as a composer and big-hearted philanthropist. She began Destin's annual art festival, and today that festival continues and features more than 80 professional artists and their creative works. And, the Mattie Kelly Arts Foundation hosts colossally cool cultural events throughout the year, such as: an annual Christmas concert, the annual World Wine Tour and Concerts in the Park (a six-week summer concert series).

It would take an entire book to feature all of the great contributions that the Kellys gave to Destin during their lifetime. And, even though they no longer live here on earth, their memory is still alive. In fact, several street signs bear their names: "Coleman's Point, Mattie's Way and Kelly Street" as a reminder of their dedication to Destin.

So, as you enjoy Destin and all of its beauty, you might send a prayer of thanks heavenward and ask God to say hello to the Kellys for you.

You'll also want to stop by the Destin Fishing Museum during your stay in this beautiful part of the country. You don't even have to be a fisherman to appreciate it!

Also on your visit, you'll want to find a book to read while relaxing on the beach. So, stop by the beautiful new library. (Two of the ladies featured on this book's cover were actually founding members of the library guild in Destin.)

Dancing Dolphins, Fabulous Fishing and Shockingly Swell Shells

Many dolphins call the Gulf their home, and they seem to be quite partial to the Destin coastline. On any given evening, you'll find dolphins jumping, playing and entertaining enthusiastic tourists. So, grab your camera and catch some dancing dolphins on film. The kids will love it!

And, for the fishermen and women in your group—Destin is the perfect vacation spot. As the "old salt" saying goes, "The "greener" the water, the bigger the fish." Attracting anglers from around the world, Destin has been deemed the "World's Luckiest Fishing Village." This tiny town boasts five saltwater world records! This is due, in part, to the 100-fathom curve, where the depth of the water reaches 600 feet (or 100-fathoms). The 100-fathom curve comes closer to Destin than any other spot in Florida, providing the quickest deep-water access on the Gulf. Do you know what that means? It means that Destin is one of the Top Five shelling destinations in the world. Also, Destin harbors the largest charter boat fleet in Florida. And, there are 24 miles of sweeping sugar sand to explore. There is an underwater treasure trove of thousands of flawless seashells. These beauties are always washing up on sand bars, white coral reefs and limestone ledges—just waiting for you to discover them and claim them as your own.

> *Fact or fiction?* A circus trapeze artist led the 2,113-passenger rescue of the luxury cruise ship Thracia—a 31,000-ton line which sank off the Northern Gulf on April 12, 1927. The circus star then opened an eclectic eatery, Harry T's Boathouse, and decorated it with his reward for his heroic actions—all the salvaged furnishings and fixtures. You decide.

Scrumptious Seafood

Do you long for fresh seafood? Does your mouth water just thinking about it? Oh yeah. Well, Destin is the place to be. Fresh Florida seafood is served by more than 400 area eateries. And, we've heard they serve at least 20 species of tasty fish on any given day—over four times more than most destinations.

If you're a seafood fanatic, you'll definitely want to take in the Destin Seafood Festival that occurs each October. This wonderful weekend kicks off the world-renowned Fishing Rodeo—a 52-year tradition of the "World's Luckiest Fishing Village" that attracts anglers from around the world for a month of frenzied fishing. The Seafood Festival is one of the highlights of the month, when more than 50,000 seafood aficionados partake in every deep-sea dish known to man—from shark kabobs to barbecued shrimp (a Texan tourist favorite!). It's a weekend of fun, food and festivities. Take in the gorgeous seascape, enjoy some magical music and mingle with the locals. It's worth your time!

Destin has an intriguing harbor enclosed by residences, dining, and condos, and of course, the fishing fleet. Every day at 4 pm, you can watch the boats come in with the "catch of the day." It's quite a sight!

SANDESTIN

Simply Sensational

If you love Destin, you'll love Sandestin, too. Here's what one reporter from the *Knoxville Sentinel* said:

"The biggest challenge our family faced at Sandestin was attempting to name the exact color of the green-tinted water. A string of gemstones came to my mind-adventure, tourmaline, apatite, fluorite, beryl." We have the answer, emerald green.

Sandestin is a place to lose yourself in the beauty of God's creation. Located just east of Destin, between Pensacola and Panama City, this award-winning resort area has something for everyone in the family. From nature parks to swimming pools to golf to sailing to tennis—Sandestin has it all! It's one of Florida's best-kept secrets, relatively unknown by much of the nation.

But, hurry! This resort area is gaining in popularity. The word is getting out! And why wouldn't it? It's gorgeous! Imagine waking up to dolphins breaking through the surface of the sea as you gaze into the morning sunlight.

Tee Time

We loved the Sandestin Golf and Beach Resort, which is known for putting the "S" back in Southern hospitality. Golfers will feel they've died and gone to Links Heaven where the motto is: "Only our guests are better cared for than our courses." With 73 amazingly unique holes, four groomed courses, and three world-renowned golf course architects—it's no wonder golfers come from around the world to test their skills and enjoy golf at one of the all-time great resorts.

Angling Opportunities

Do you love to fish? Pompano fishing is one of the great phenomena of Sandestin. During the spring and early fall of each year, anglers surf cast and pull in pompano by the buckets full, using sand fleas for bait. Just don't get caught trying to catch any loggerhead or leatherback sea turtles. The locals are quite fond of their little turtle friends. These turtles are on the endangered species list, and Florida is home to the largest population of nesting sea turtles in the United States. In fact, the Sandestinites are so fond of their turtle friends that they watch over the nests, monitoring them until the hatchlings make it safely into the sea. It's really something to see…

Make Sandestin a vacation destination for your next get-away…emerald green water and white beaches are calling your name!

Destin/Sandestin—Shopping Sensations

Destin shopping delights are around every corner, down every street, and in places you'd never expect. The variety will impress even the most seasoned shopper. From first-class to funky, it can all be found in Destin.

Shoppers will adore the charming shops and boutiques found in the Village of Baytowne Wharf—the heart and soul of Sandestin. You'll experience strolling musicians, street performers, sunset celebrations and the aroma of baking bread coming from the Village Bakery. Trust us, your senses will be overloaded to the point of ecstasy.

DID YOU KNOW?

- that pop star Britney Spears owns a condo in Destin?
- that author John Grisham lives on Holiday Isle in Destin part of the year?
- that Jeff Cook, a member of the legendary country music group Alabama, lives in Destin?

For more information on Destin, call the Destin Chamber of Commerce at 850-837-6241 or visit www.destinchamber.com/ online.

For more information on Sandestin, visit Beaches of South Walton at www.beachesofsouthwalton.com online or call 800-822-6877 or 850-267-1216.

Destin/Sandestin Fairs Festivals & Fun

January
Great Southern Gumbo Cookoff
Snowbird Activities Galore

February
American Heart Ball
Carnivale By The Sea
Boat Show

March
Cobia World Tournament
Easter Egg Hunts
Home Show
Florida Sportsman Fishing Show
Boggy Bayou Golf Classic

April
St. Mary's Spring Fling
Sandestin Wine Tasting
March of Dimes, Walk America
Emerald Coast Golf Tournament

May
Arts Quest
Miss Destin Pageant
Billy Bowlegs Golf Tournament
Pinfish Classic
Gate to Gate Run-Eglin AFB
Memorial Day Concert
Blessing of the Fleet

June
Billy Bowlegs Festival
Concert Series-Mattie Kelly Arts Foundation
One Design Summer Regatta

July
Fireworks, East Pass
Open Spearfishing Competition
Sportfish Tournament
Concert Series-Mattie Kelly Arts Foundation

August
Concert Series - Market at Sandestin
Rally for Recreation
Annual Elephant Walk Triathlon
King Mackerel Tournament
Dog Days Open Billfish Tour
Art & Experience Auction

September
Concert Series - Market at Sandestin
Labor Day Concerts/Celebration
Open Spearfishing-Fantasea Scuba
Shoot Out, Fishing Rodeo

October
Destin Seafood Festival
Destin Fishing Rodeo
Destin Festival of the Arts
Halloween @ Silver Sands Factory Stores
Star Chef, March of Dimes
Best of the Emerald Coast, March of Dimes

November
Emerald Coast Golf Tour
Great Gulf Coast Arts Festival
Don Sutton Celebrity Golf Tournament
Zoo Lights
Fall Concert Series
Holiday on the Harbor

December
Destin Christmas Parade
Destin Christmas Boat Parade
World Wine Tour
The Sounds of the Season

BIENVENUE VINTAGE HOME

Ann Miller Hopkins and her adorable, cuddly pup named BeBe say, "Bienvenue," to their eclectic collection of wonderful antiques and vintage architectural objects. First-time visitors to Bienvenue Vintage Home, at 11840 Hwy. 98 W., are amazed when they walk through the doors of the huge  metal warehouse. Inside are vignettes displaying incredible vintage furniture and antiques from across the nation and Europe. The Hopkins travel to Paris and the South of France several times a year to shop flea markets and scour the countryside for architectural antiques, vintage doors, windows, stained glass and rustic wrought-iron pieces. Bienvenue carries many large entry pieces and antique chandeliers, as well as collectible vintage pottery. Wander through 6,000 square feet of garden furniture, nautical elements, antique books, jewelry, vintage lighting, estate china and linens. You have to see it to believe it! "We give you old money style on a budget," says Ann. (Large and small budgets welcome!) Hours are Monday-Saturday 10 am-5 pm and Sunday 1-5 pm. Call 850-837-5122. Oh, by the way, "Bienvenue" means Welcome!

CLEMENTS ANTIQUES
OF FLORIDA, INC.

Photo by imagephasinc.com

Sandra Clements learned the antique business literally from the "floor" up. Her father, Wallace Clements, was a pioneer in the antique business and the first person to bring an entire container of English antiques to the United States. As the Clements family traveled throughout the country looking for unusual and valuable pieces, Sandra and her four siblings worked right alongside their parents, scouting for treasures, wrapping the glassware, and packing the truck. She even assisted her parents with their very first auction. Wallace Clements was the auctioneer, his wife Doris clerked, her sister Brenda cashiered, and Sandra "worked the floor."

In 1989, Sandra fulfilled her long-time dream of owning and operating her own antique store. Clements Antiques of Florida, 9501 U.S. Hwy. 98 W., is a beautiful place filled with 17th, 18th, 19th, and 20th century American, English, French and Continental furniture, oil paintings, porcelain, silver accessories, bronze statuary, and works of art. The shop also boasts some of the finest quality new items such as Baccarat; frames by Jay Strongwater; Lalique; Waterford crystal; fabulous handmade rugs; and one-of-a-kind English and French reproduction furniture.

One intangible that makes Clements Antiques such a fantastic place is the effervescent Ms. Clements herself. Sandra is an engaging lady with a contagious smile and a love for life. She has followed in the footsteps of her parents, and is a master auctioneer, making every auction an enjoyable event with her considerable wit and humor.

Allow plenty of time to leisurely wander through Sandra's vast array of beautiful and unique items. You'll find the perfect piece that will not only be a reminder of your trip to Destin, but also a wonderful treasure for your home. The store is open Monday-Saturday 9 am-5 pm. Call 850-837-1374. *(Color picture featured in front section of the book.)*

Flutterby
ANTIQUES
UNIQUES & GIFTS

When Ron Sandstead and Michele Steiner bought a warehouse full of "stuff" from a good friend, they had no idea where it would lead. But after spending eight days in the July heat packing and loading everything into a 48-foot semitrailor, they did know one thing—they were officially in the "antique business!" Flutterby Antiques, Uniques & Gifts at 211 Main St. in Destin is a cheerful shop full of hidden treasures. You'll find a wonderful combination of American-made furniture, some primitives, and lots of European pieces. Michele specifically collects ceramic teapots and pottery, while Ron loves old hand-colored lithographs and antique tools. You'll discover homey, eclectic "stuff" in every corner, and inventory changes often. Be sure to ask about the story behind the store's charming name. Open Tuesday-Saturday 10 am-5 pm or by appointment. Visit online www.cobaltflutterby@cox.net or call 850-269-3200.

SMITH'S ANTIQUES MALL

When Nedra and Hugh Smith moved from Washington, D.C. and retired to Sandestin in 1993, they missed the international market quality of collectibles and antiques they had been accustomed to finding. So, they opened Smith's Antiques Mall at 12500 Emerald Coast Pkwy., which has become one of the premier antique malls in the country. Voted "Best on the Emerald Coast" year after year, *Southern Accents* has listed it as a "must-do" when visiting Destin. Make it your first place to shop for incredible antiques, gifts and collectibles. Hours are Monday-Saturday 10 am-6 pm, Tuesday until 10 pm and Sunday noon-5 pm. Call 850-654-1484.

Artists, Art Galleries, Framing & Photography

Beverly McNeil is the owner of Portrait Brokers of America, which represents more than 100 of the nation's finest portrait artists, and helps clients match the right artist with their individual preferences. Her many years in the art world paved the way for the opening of this wonderful Destin art gallery in Signature Studios, 36062 Emerald Coast Pkwy. The studio offers a diverse inventory of artwork and showcases a wide range of periods, styles, and subject matter. You'll find original works in oil, pastel, watercolor, and sculpture by leading artists, as well as 19th century antique English paintings and portraits. And, you will love the eclectic mix, from the whimsical to the traditional paintings of the past. Beverly travels to England often in search of the best sources for antique paintings and portraits. Art lovers will definitely want to make this a stop. The gallery is open Monday-Saturday 10:30 am-5:30 pm. Check for upcoming gallery events and receptions by calling 850-654-4322 or by visiting www.beverlymcneil.com online. *(Color picture featured in front section of the book.)*

PAGE O'CONNOR
FINE ARTS
INCORPORATED

Working on the premise that "artwork is the heart of the home's decor," Page O'Connor has helped furnish some of the most beautiful homes on the Emerald Coast. Her motto, "You can buy a picture to match your sofa. . . or you can buy a piece of Art to match your Soul," describes her commitment to helping customers find their signature piece of art—something that truly speaks to them on a personal level. Page made her long-time dream come true in opening Page O'Connor Fine Arts, Inc. at 8955 Hwy. 98 W. in Destin. Once you've chosen that perfect piece, she encourages you to choose your framing carefully. Excellent framing can

add much to the image you fell in love with, and increase its value. Page is extremely knowledgeable, very confident and great fun. The shop is open Monday-Friday 9 am-6 pm and Saturday 'til 4 pm. Call 850-267-8433 or visit www.pageoconnorfineart.com for more information.

Because she grew up on the beautiful Destin coastline, Iris Freshwater shares its beauty as a backdrop for many of her award-winning photographs. She has been in the personal imaging business for more than 25 years, which includes make-up, photography, and hand-tinted portraits. View her many accomplishments in the field of both black and white and color photography at www.imagesbyiris.com online. For more information, call 850-837-9057 or 850-865-1868.

"PORTRAITS IN OIL" BY LEIGH SEALY

Inspired and encouraged by her mother, Leigh Sealy attended Ringling School of Art & Design in Sarasota, and then returned to Destin to hone her talent in portrait art. Her works include one-of-a-kind portrait and figure art, featuring original portraits of Elvis Presley, Marilyn Monroe, John Wayne, John Lennon, and an autographed original of B.B. King! She works from her studio condo that overlooks the Gulf, and can be reached for an appointment at 850-837-3675.

You have seen his work in *Southern Living Magazine*, *Veranda*, and *Architectural Digest*. He has one of the most successful faux finish and restoration businesses from Atlanta to Destin, and is a name spoken all along the Emerald Coast. Robert Kersey is a master at restoration art, with an authenticity that truly sets him apart in his field.

Robert pays attention to trends in paint finishes, elaborates on trends, even starts many trends, but puts his definitive mark on every project. From the popular metallic "institutional" finishes that are so popular right now, to tropical bamboo walls, or a Tuscan stone texture, the artists at Kersey & Co. will transform your ordinary rooms into memorable masterpieces. Kersey's talent with paint finishes is remarkable, but he is also a talented potter. He has created replica bowl sinks with beautiful finishings for kitchens and baths. This is simply home décor at its best. Contact Kersey & Co. for a tour of the current project. For more information or an appointment, visit www.kerseyandcompany.com or call 850-830-3033.

FINE PORTRAIT PHOTOGRAPHY

Captivated by the image of her six-month-old son playing with an uprooted marigold, Trish Waddle was inspired to take a picture of that precious moment. That photo session awakened a passion in her that has transpired into a very successful career with her Portrait Photography by Trish.

Moving from Atlanta to Florida, Trish has found the beach to be the perfect background for the elegant look of her pictures. She specializes in family, children, babies, and mother-and-baby portraits. An award-winning photographer, Trish uses natural lighting and the beauty of nature to record the purest moments for each customer. Portrait Photography by Trish, 120 Benning Dr., continues to be the most creative way to preserve families' special moments.

For more information or to make an appointment, call 850-837-6614.

BEAU-ESPRIT GALLERY

The name means "Good Spirit," which perfectly describes the ambiance of this very sophisticated and beautiful gallery and frame shop at 4424 Commons Dr. E, #3-A in Destin. Lovely music welcomes you into the gallery, which is a colorful treat for the eyes, featuring original art, beautiful prints, and wonderful gifts for the home. An artist herself, Stacy Barrett loves being able to use her artistic talents to design frames for artwork, mirrors, or family photos. With more than 1500 frame selections and hundreds of mat choices, the possibilities are endless! Hours are Monday-Saturday 10 am-5 pm. Call 850-837-2757 or visit www.beau-esprit.com online.

DEEP SEA FISHING
WITH SUNRISE CHARTERS

Captain Kelly Windes has been a fisherman all of his life. In fact, much to his parents' dismay, his Uncle Irby used to pick him up at the bus stop before school, and they would fish all day! After graduating from high school, Kelly joined the Navy, where as a Quartermaster, he found himself navigating a 300-foot warship during the Vietnam War. When he returned to Destin, it didn't take him long to purchase his own boat to begin his life in the fishing industry. Today, Kelly owns and runs Sunrise Charters, and holds several world and state all-tackle records!

Capt. Kelly Windes' "Charter Boat Sunrise" lifts anchor from the Destin Fishing Fleet Marina located right behind the Fisherman's Wharf Restaurant, a half mile east of the Destin Bridge. His charter business started in 1981 with Charter Boat Sunrise. He has since partnered with and added Capt. Eric Thrasher on Daybreak; Capt. Steve Haeusler on First Light; Capt. Robert Hill on Twilight; and Capt. Mark Hanshaw on Summer Wind. All boats are fast, clean, comfortable, and air-conditioned. They also feature interior bunks, dining areas, and restrooms. You bring the snacks and your captain and mate will supply the bait, ice, tackle, fishing licenses, and of course, the perfect spots for the best fish-

ing of your life! You may also reserve one of the most popular party boats—the Destin Princess—for year round fishing excursions or reserve the Sweetheart for dolphin and sunset cruises, weddings or special parties.

Besides being the most recognized charter boat captain in the area, Kelly is something of a reluctant hero to the fishermen in Destin. As the city grew, and the coastland became more valuable, the local fishing marinas were in danger of being bought up by hungry land developers. With much foresight, countless man-hours, and lots of determination, Kelly put together a small group of independent, very headstrong fishermen. Together, they were able to close a deal with a landowner for a long strip of waterfront property for what has become the Destin Fishing Fleet Marina, home and security for 40 professional, recreational fishing boats. Although he constantly gives credit to those around him, locals recognize that it was his vision, leadership, and faith that held the project together. The marina is hailed today as a "Model Marina" in the state of Florida. Tourists and locals alike love to watch the boats come in with the huge catches of fish. Open seven days a week, call Sunrise Charters for information, schedules, or reservations at 850-837-2320 or visit www.destin-charter-fishing.com online.

THE SAILING SCHOONER
DANIEL WEBSTER CLEMENTS

Bill Campbell often dreamed of building a historically authentic wooden sailing schooner—one that would reflect the nautical heritage of the area, as well as express the ideas he loved about sailing. Bill acquired photographs and drawings of a historic schooner from the Smithsonian Institute and procured the services of a wooden boat builder in Coden, Ala.—then began the hard work to transform dream into reality. Four years later, Bill launched and commissioned his sailing schooner, the *Daniel Webster Clements*, named in honor of his wife Dianne's father, Dan Clements, a life-long high school principal. With an amazing crew of friends and family, the *Daniel Webster Clements* has become a maritime institution in Destin.

As a member of the American Sail Training Association, the Clements has found its niche in providing weeklong adventure programs for youth. Bill and crew also offer a unique "on-board" nautical classroom—teaching children navigation, science, and history in rotating learning stations right on deck.

When in port, the *Clements* regularly takes visitors on afternoon and evening sails into the Gulf and into Choctawhatchee Bay. You'll love the "sunset dolphin" cruises and the "snorkel *and* sail" cruises! They get lots of requests for wedding ceremonies to be performed by the ship's Captain while undersail. Because of the *Clements'* roomy, stable decks and romantic appeal, she is the perfect setting for reunions, parties and business occasions.

For information or reservations aboard the schooner *Daniel Webster Clements*, visit www.sailingsouth.com online or call 850-837-7245.

KELLY PLANTATION

Blessed with miles of deep-water shoreline, towering trees and intricate bayous, Kelly Plantation is a virtual paradise of nature's goodness. It is Destin's most exclusive residential golf club community, and its history is as poignantly beautiful as the land itself. Mattie and Coleman Kelly bought the property in 1930, and established a turpentine farm, which flourished for more than 40 years as one of Destin's leading industries. After closing the turpentine facility, Mattie Kelly vowed to fulfill her late husband's dream of turning this extraordinary setting into something very special. Partners Davage Runnels, Jr. and John A. McNeil, Jr. have created what they call "the masterpiece on the bay," and have honored the wishes and dreams of two of Destin's most memorable citizens.

Kelly Plantation is located at 4393 Commons Dr. E. in Destin, between the Choctawhatchee Bay and the Gulf of Mexico. There are a limited number of homesites available in the Plantation, where families can enjoy the beauty of the nature trails, lakes, parks and bayous. And, if you're a golfer, you'll think you've died and gone to heaven. Kelly Plantation features a magnificent 18-hole Fred Couples golf course. Its par 72, 7,099-yard course offers some of the most challenging golf found anywhere, and is considered by sports writers to be "the brightest gem in the Emerald Coast setting." The course stretches over 200 acres bordering the bay. Inside the distinctive clubhouse, the Members' Grill serves lunch daily and is available for special events and occasions. Combine this with the dramatic lawns that frame the clubhouse, and you have the perfect location for a wedding and/or reception, a birthday party or a baby shower. For information on this remarkable golf community, visit www.kellyplantation.com online or call 850-650-7600 or 800-837-5080. It is truly a place unlike any other!

THE GOLF GARDEN
Family Golf Center

Ten years ago, when a pristine land site along Emerald Coast Parkway became available, the need for affordable golf was met with the creation of The Golf Garden Family Golf Center. Today, it is the premiere family spot for golf, featuring an executive golf course, a driving range, and an 18-hole putting course. All levels and ages are welcome!

Located at 12958 Emerald Coast Pkwy. in Destin, you'll find a friendly, relaxed atmosphere in the Garden clubhouse, where expansive windows overlook the courses. Relax and enjoy a snack or beverage before your tee time—refreshments are available from 7:30 am and continue late during the summer months, when the

course is illuminated for nighttime play. If you need instruction, a PGA Pro is on staff to give lessons. Open daily 7:30 am to 5 pm, September through May, and 7:30 am to 11 pm, June through August. Call 850-837-7422.

Today's mighty oak
is just yesterday's nut
that held its ground.

—Unknown

Bakeries & Ice Cream Parlors

At age 16, Kim Weideman made her first real cake—a Darth Vader design for her brother's birthday. From that moment on her life has become even "sweeter." Today, people come from miles around to visit her charming Southern Style Bakery at 114 Palmetto St. #12 in Destin. Stop by and see her scrumptious goodies, then you'll know why Kim is known as the "cake lady" and the bakery has been voted best on the Emerald Coast. Open Tuesday-Friday 9 am-5 pm and Saturday til noon. Call 850-654-1716 or visit www.southernstyledesserts.com.

They call it, "An Arctic Sensation in a Sunny Location!" We call it the sweetest treat in town. Penguin's Ice Cream is located in the Village of Baytowne Wharf at Sandestin Resort, 9300 Emerald Coast Pkwy. Enjoy gourmet ice cream including very vanilla, milk and dark chocolates, and a variety of delicious flavors. Create your own flavors from more than 20 awesome "mix-in" choices that are cut into your ice cream on a marble slab as you watch. Call 850-351-1809 for store hours.

You'll hear words like "romantic, elegant, quaint, charming, graceful, and serene" used to describe Florida's premiere bed and breakfast—Henderson Park Inn. It is the perfect blend of beachside elegance and beauty, with more than a mile of untouched silver beaches and glittering gulf views. The architecture is "Old New England" with old-fashioned Victorian reproduction furnishings.

You'll enjoy luxuriant bathrobes; cable TV; in-room safes; fresh coffee; and daily maid service. Plus, most rooms feature a Jacuzzi; a refrigerator; an icemaker; and a microwave. A complimentary true Southern-style breakfast is served each morning, and "The Veranda" dining room is open each day for lunch and Tuesday-Saturday for dinner. The inn, 2700 Scenic Hwy. 98 in Destin, is open 24 hours daily. Call 850-654-0400 or 800-336-4853 or visit www.hendersonparkinn.com online.

INN
ON DESTIN
HARBOR

After living short stints in Scottsdale, Ariz. and Atlanta, Ga., Patti and Charles Noonan were drawn back to their favorite place in the world—Destin. When the chance to buy the charming Inn on Destin Harbor presented itself, they knew that it would be the perfect opportunity to come be an integral part of the place they loved so much. The Inn has a wonderful history. It was formerly a famous breakfast spot for Destin's local "who's who," boat captains, and civic leaders.

You will love the cozy, intimate feeling of the Inn, tucked high atop a bluff overlooking the Destin Harbor and East Pass. It has been called a "small boutique hotel," mainly because of its impeccable service and attention to detail. Concierge service is available to guests 24 hours a day, and a wonderful continental breakfast is served each morning in the great room. Here you'll find a cozy fireplace overlooking the water—a beautiful place to gather with friends for coffee or a glass of wine. There are 41 rooms—with a breathtaking view of the harbor, especially at sunset! You'll find a harbor-front pool and private harbor beach adjacent to the pool.

And, you'll be within walking distance of award-winning restaurants such as Marina Café, Destin Chops, A.J.'s and Harbor Docks, and only a short water-taxi ride from The Gulf of Mexico. The Inn at 402 Harbor Blvd. on Destin Harbor is an elegant and private retreat. The ambience is charming! Room amenities include private balconies, mini refrigerators, hair dryers, and coffee and tea makers. The staff is incredibly friendly and accommodating. For more information or reservations, call 850-837-7326 or visit www.innondestinharbor.com. *(Color picture featured in front section of the book.)*

DESTIN

Marcia and Tommy Green believe that "God does not call the equipped, He equips the called, and as usual, goes far beyond your expectations." When Tommy's brother called him with a suggestion that he and Marcia open a restaurant in Destin similar to the one he owned in Mandeville, La., the couple prayed about it, and then jumped right into the frying pan—sunny side up! Another Broken Egg Café at 104 Hwy. 98 has won "Best Breakfast on the Emerald Coast" four years in a row, and has been featured in *Southern Living Magazine*. You'll enjoy a vast array of omelets from a traditional flavor to a saucy Southwestern flair, as well as popular Eggs Benedict, and Country Sausage and Gravy. Another Broken Egg Café is perhaps most famous for its spectacular Bananas Foster. Breakfast is served all day if you wish, but lunches are a treat with homemade hamburgers, deli sandwiches and exceptional salads. Mix together bright, appealing charm; a pleasing atmosphere; large doses of smiling, friendly servers; and generous quantities of delicious edibles; and you have a recipe for Another Broken Egg Café! Hours are Tuesday-Sunday 7 am-2 pm. Call 850-650-0499.

There aren't many restaurants with the charm of an old winery, an impressive wine list, a world-renowned chef, and a classy, yet relaxed casual family atmosphere. Cuvée Beach has it all! The beautiful building at 36120 Emerald Coast Pkwy. in Destin features an incomparable retail wine cellar and a full bar with excellent martinis. Cuvée Beach is the culmination of a long-time dream for four friends (three from Mississippi) who love great food and wine. Doctors Bill and Ann Dent, and Dr. Phillip and Brenda Nunnery have done an extraordinary job creating this wonderful restaurant and wine cellar. Chef Steven Alex Vanderpool masterfully prepares "wine country cuisine with a gulf twist" in the exhibition

kitchen nightly. They offer 40 wines by the glass and wine experts to help you find the perfect wine for your taste and budget. Catering and private party rooms are available. Call 850-650-8900 or visit www.cuveebeach.com.

MISS CHEN TAIWANESE RESTAURANT

If you're hungry, but not sure what you're in the mood for, stop into Miss Chen's Authentic Taiwanese Restaurant and ask the expert—Miss Chen herself. Just tell her your favorite ingredients and get ready for a taste bud sensation. Located directly across from the harbor, 107 Hwy. 98 E., Miss Chen is also known for her hook 'em and cook 'em recipes—simply bring in your fresh catch and sit back as she cooks it to perfection. For more information and hours, call 850-837-2311.

When people ask Jere or Marcy Boutz the question, "Seafood in a Mexican restaurant?" they remind them that after all, the Gulf is the "Gulf of Mexico. La Paz, 950 Gulf Shore Dr. in Destin, is a colorful Mexican restaurant decorated in the warm Santa Fe style, featuring southwestern cuisine and coastal Mexican seafood dishes. Taking advantage of all of the wonderful gifts from the sea, they prepare shrimp and crab dishes with a zesty Mexican twist. Of course, you will also find traditional Mexican dishes and

tasty salsas. Make sure you sample the house favoritesGouper or Tuna Burritos and the Shrimp Stuffed Poblano Chilus! La Paz is always voted one of the top "Mexican" restaurants on the Emerald Coast. Stop by and see why! It is open for lunch 11 am-2 pm and for dinner 5-10 pm Monday-Friday, Saturday 11 am-10 pm and Sunday noon-10pm. Call 850-837-2247.

RESTAURANT / BAR

& GOVERNOR'S ATTIC LOUNGE

There is a spectacular world just inside this incredible Gulf-front Destin restaurant. The Elephant Walk, 9300 Emerald Coast Pkwy. W., is an exotic dining adventure. From USDA Prime Steaks and Pan-seared Grouper to Lump Crab Cakes and Pepper-grilled Mahi Mahi, everything is perfect! The multi-leveled restaurant is home to The Governor's Attic lounge upstairs–what a view! Open daily at 6 pm during summer and 5 pm during winter. Call 850-267-4800.

You might have glimpsed a bit of the original Hog's Breath Café in a scene from the 1970's movie "Jaws 2." Or, you might have recognized it as the background setting for MTV's annual "Homemade Bikini Contest!" Or . . . you might have seen the Hog's Breath T-shirt sported in the major motion picture "Something About Mary." So, what is Hog's Breath? Well, it is one of the most popular and best-loved restaurants and saloons in all of Florida. Jerry Dorminy established the Original Hog's Breath Saloon in 1976 in Fort Walton Beach. It was a place where he and his friends could "hang out" after a full day of fishing or sailing. It fast became a favorite watering hole and family-style restaurant for locals and visitors alike. And, in 1988 a second location was established in Key West, Fla. When Hurricane Opal almost demolished the café in 1995, Jerry decided to relocate to Destin, and its popularity has continued to grow. No longer the original "beach bar concept," Hog's Breath is all about family—great food, good music, cool atmosphere, and lots of familiar faces.

One of the things visitors love the most (in addition to the fabulous food) is the live webcast—an audio and visual opportunity to engage in "Hog Breath fun." The little Hog's Breath T-shirt booth has grown into a large clothing store, featuring a full array of clothing, located next door to the café. Visit Hog's Breath online at www.hogsbreath.com for the great T-shirts, sweatshirts, hats, and gifts. The café is located at 541 Hwy. 98 E. and is open Sunday-Thursday 11 am-11 pm and Friday-Saturday 11 am-12 am. For more information, call 850-837-5991 or 800-826-6969.

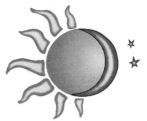

SOLEIL et LUNA

Restaurant and Lounge

Although Soleil et Luna, 747 Hwy. 98 in Destin, is known for its fabulous food, its eclectic beauty has created quite a buzz. It all begins outside the restaurant with the incredible mosaic fashioned from everything you can imagine—sunglasses, broken dishes, beaded necklaces—it is quite a piece of art. The owners' passion for food, color, and art are evident. Todd and Sabrina Reber and Chef John Jacob are partners in this remarkable restaurant, which is known to have consistently fresh and creative cuisine and hands-on personal service. New additions to Soleil et Luna include Chef John's Takeaway Gourmet, award-winning gourmet specialty foods, and cleverly designed baskets and corporate gifts. There is also a catering team equipped to meet any special event need. Open daily 11 am-2 am. Be sure to visit www.soleiletluna.com online for more information, or call 850-650-0332.

THE

Grille

AT
SILVER SHELLLS

Reward yourself with an award-winning meal at The Grille at Silver Shells, 15000 Emerald Coast Pkwy. in Destin. Guests of both Silver Shells Beach Resort and Silver Beach Towers have access to some of the most incredible cuisine in Florida in a casual dining setting. Chef Chris Chirum certainly has a "silver" touch, with delectable creations such as Brandied Lobster Bisque, Choctawhatchee Bay Crab Cakes, and Portobello Mushroom Napoleon—and those are just the appetizers! Wonderful entrees include Almond Crusted Mahi Mahi, Grouper St. Thomas, Braised Lamb Shank, and Ginger Snap Duck Breast. An extensive wine list compliments the dinner creations, and the desserts are all homemade. The Grille is also the perfect location for beach ceremonies, wedding receptions, holiday parties, and other special occasions. Open 11:30 am-9 pm. Visit www.silvershells.com or call 850-337-5108. *(Color picture featured in front section of the book.)*

CIAO BELLA PIZZA

Ali Bulutoglu and his wife Charlotte swear by their homemade bread and garlic dip that's "to die for," and are known to make a pretty tasty pie...pizza pie, that is. Ciao Bella Pizza, 29 Hwy. 98 E. in Destin, is a laid-back eatery with unforgettable food and a fun, unique atmosphere—whether you choose to dine in with beautiful Italian music setting the mood or outside overlooking the Destin Harbor. Open Monday-Saturday 11 am-10 pm and Sunday 1-10 pm. Call 850-654-9815.

The Boathouse Oyster Bar, 288 Hwy. 98 E., is a "landmark" Destin restaurant. Locals love it! In fact, it has been voted "best gumbo" for several years running as well as "Best on the Emerald Coast." Wanda "Mama Gumbo" Green and Paul "Action" Jackson started the business in 1986. The building was originally a boathouse that was built in the 1940s, so the oyster bar is located on the harbor and has a breathtaking view. All over the walls and rafters, you'll find a mosaic of dollar bills, bikinis, auto tags, and other items that people have stapled over the years to leave their mark. Who knows? You may want to staple something yourself!

As you might have guessed by the nickname of the owners, The Boathouse is well known for its fabulous gumbo. The menu also includes other things like raw oysters of course, but also baked oysters; hot wings; and a variety of sandwiches. It's simply a great place to enjoy a cold beer, and there is live entertainment seven nights a week and in the afternoon on Friday-Sunday. Hours are 11 am-'til . . . every day—closed in the month of December and only open Friday-Sunday in January and February. Call 850-837-3645.

M·U·L·H·O·L·L·O·W·S BiSTRO 2·1·5

Everything about the eclectic sidewalk café, and unique bistro, is wonderful. The café and bistro are a perfect blend of cultures, taste, and atmosphere. And, both are the result of two very talented people doing what they absolutely love—cooking! Even the names are a delightful combination of the last two names of the owners, Susan Mullaney and Matt Penhollow. The sidewalk café resembles a back alley in France, with facades that look like buildings on either wall. The bistro was modeled after a New York wine bar—very industrial, but with soft colors and bamboo. In keeping with the unique atmosphere of the restaurants, the food itself is a wonderful mix. You'll enjoy spicy Cajun and Caribbean specialties, and everything is infused with a Eurasian flair. The salads are incredible—especially the one made with Thai curry chicken, mango, spinach, and grilled bananas. Matt says that he "accidentally" read the recipe wrong and grilled bananas instead of banana peppers, but it was so delicious, it has become their best seller! These places are sure to become your favorites. Hours for the cafe, in Destin at 4424 Commons Dr. E. #3-C, are Monday-Thursday 11 am-4 pm and Friday-Saturday 11 am-9 pm; and the bistro, in Fort Walton Beach at 215 Miracle Strip Pkwy., Monday-Saturday 11 am-10 pm. Call the café at 850-269-0185 or the bistro at 850-796-3663.

Sunset Bay Café

The best way to describe this wonderful bay eatery is "resort casual dining with a Caribbean flare." Located at 9300 Emerald Coast Pkwy., Sunset Bay Café serves breakfast, lunch, and dinner from 6:30 am–9 pm. Local favorites are the "Friday Night Fish Fry" and Prime Time Saturday Night, featuring mouthwatering prime rib. You will love the food, the beautiful bay views, and the friendly owners. Call 850-267-7108 or visit www.sandestin.com. online.

If you're looking for great seafood, a casual family setting, and an outstanding view of the Gulf of Mexico, head on out to The Crab Trap, 3500 Scenic Hwy. 98 E. directly on the beach in Destin.

The Crab Trap offers affordable prices and a fun atmosphere. You can dine in the main room or try the open air Boiler Room deck. Also, the new Tiki Bar, only a few feet from the water's edge, is fantastic for Gulf gazing or people watching.

The menu here is extensive. Try the Alaskan snow crab, King crab and Dungeness crab, as well as crab cakes, she crab soup, crab claws and crab dip or, enjoy jumbo Gulf white shrimp prepared chargrilled, boiled, blackened, fried or scampi style. Fresh fish is always abundant with at least five species served daily. The Crab Trap hours are 11 am-11 pm, daily. For more information, call 850-654-2722.

If you had only one night to spend in Destin, the Ocean Club Restaurant and Bar would be the perfect place. This first-class restaurant combines great food, service, and live entertainment into one room. David Seering, an amazing pianist and vocalist has provided entertainment at the Ocean Club since 1993. Year after year, David has been chosen the most outstanding entertainer on the Emerald Coast and his musical repertoire spans from Broadway tunes to Big Band hits. It's no wonder the Ocean Club is chosen repeatedly by patrons as #1 in fine dining and entertainment. Locals feel it is "the" place to be seen in Destin. The menu has a New Orleans (Continental) influence, offering all the local seafood, including Grouper, Snapper, soft shell crab and Lump Crabmeat. Of course, the seafood is always the freshest. There is a children's menu, too. The Ocean Club, 8955 Hwy. 98 W. #107, is open daily for dinner at 5 pm. For more information, call 850-267-3666 or visit www.oceanclubdestin.com online.

Back in 1979, Harbor Docks was a weather-beaten little cottage with six picnic tables, cold beer, and fresh oysters on the half shell. The spectacular view of the harbor is the same, but over the years owner Charles Morgan has added—a sushi bar, a hibachi grill, and a deck that sprawls along the waterfront. His made-from-scratch food is delicious and healthy, including gumbo, red beans and rice, crab claws, boiled shrimp, and of course, fresh oysters on the half shell! The restaurant is also well known for its Thai dishes, including spring rolls made with chicken and vegetables, served with a sweet chili sauce. Breakfast is served 5:30-10:30 am, lunch 11 am-4 pm; and dinner 5-11 pm every day. Catering is available for special events or private parties. Harbor Docks, 538 Hwy. 98 in Destin, offers a wonderful view of the dock, delicious seafood, and the opportunity to soak up a little local flavor. For more information, call 850-837-2506.

CALLAHAN'S RESTAURANT & DELI

If you ask the Destin locals where to go for great food, they will send you to Callahan's Restaurant & Deli. A long-time local favorite, Callahan's was voted "Best Value," "Best Salad," "Best Casual Dining," and "Best Deli Sandwich/Eatery" in the *"Best of the Emerald Coast."*

Locals know they can count on getting great meals at great prices. The menu has a wide variety of soups, salads, sandwiches and entrees including steaks, seafood, chicken, pasta, and more. In addition to the marvelous menu, Callahan's also features daily lunch and dinner specials.

You will find Callahan's in the heart of Destin at 950 Gulf Shore Dr. Open Monday-Friday 10 am to 9-10 pm and Saturday 8 am to 9-10 pm. Call 850-837-7171 for more information.

SANDESTIN

When Ron Green decided to move "back home" to his Southern roots in 1992, he realized that he missed his favorite little California café called The Good Egg. "Why not take the concept south?" he asked, and The Broken Egg Café was hatched in Mandeville, LA. And, its success was phenomenal. Building upon the reputation of its wonderful menu and great customer service, he with the help of his wife Sharon, opened four other Another Broken Egg Cafés with the last one at 9100 Baytowne Wharf in Sandestin. Breakfast is the most important meal of the day at Another Broken Egg Café! Gourmet "scratch" pancakes with whipped butter and warm syrup, Eggs Benedict, Blackberry Grits, and Southern Biscuits and Gravy are just a few of the wonderful items on the menu. Brunch and lunch items are also "eggcellent!" The café is open daily 7:00 am-3 pm. Call 850-622-2050 for more "eggcellent" info!

The true test of whether a Mexican restaurant is worth its margarita salt is determined by two important things—great margaritas, and great chips and salsa. Cancun's Mexican Restaurant, 12889 Emerald Coast Pkwy in Destin, can boast that both are excellent! In fact, the restaurant's margaritas, and chips and salsa have been voted "Best of the Emerald Coast," by *Emerald Coast Magazine*.

The atmosphere is casual and fun, with live entertainment every weekend. The restaurant comes alive with music, laughter, and song, which make the food even tastier! The bright, pleasing colors of the décor; the sweet, friendly attention from the staff; and the delicious Mexican fare: guarantee a wonderful dining experience for both locals and visitors. It is open Sunday-Thursday 11 am-9 pm, and Friday-Saturday until 10 pm. For more information, call 850-269-7788.

MAGNOLIA & IVY

Be sure and check out Magnolia & Ivy in the Tearooms section of the Destin chapter. See page 81 for full details.

NOT FISHY COOKING TIPS

The biggest mistake is overcooking!!! Cook a minute or two under the time specified in most cookbooks and then check—you can always cook more. Whole or filleted fish will easily separate with a fork when it's done. The rule of thumb for estimating quantity is 1/2 of a pound per person.

—Peggy Adams

Children's Shops

You will feel as though you've stepped back into your own childhood days when you visit Toys & Treasures at 9375 Emerald Coast Pkwy. W. in the Sandestin Market Shops. This little hands-on, kid-friendly toy store is filled with treasures like Madame Alexander dolls, Playmobile, Groovy Girls, Thomas the Tank Trains, and pink toile ballerina costumes. Open spring and summer 10 am-9 pm and 10 am-6 pm fall and winter. Call 850-267-6550 or visit www.toysandtreasures.net.

The Destin locals say that they are SOOO excited to have this wonderful children's shop in the area. After one peek inside, you will also be enthralled with the charm and excitement of Brat'z, 34904 Emerald Coast Pkwy. It almost shouts fun and celebration with its brightly-painted walls and floors, and the clever and creative displays of bright green raincoats and umbrellas. Brat'z is the brain-child of Cheryl Chamblee, who is also the owner of "Girl Friendz" located in the same center. The counter is painted with pink poodles, and the floors with games such as "Twister," so that children are thoroughly entertained while mom shops. In addition children can watch cartoons in the entertainment video area, or play with the many hands-on educational toys for sale. The clothing ranges in size from infant to pre-teen, and the styles are very trendy and popular with "fashion princesses" who are in the know. Brat'z store hours are Monday-Saturday 10 am-7 pm and Sunday 12pm-5 pm. Call 850-650-5477 for more information.

THE RESORTS OF
PELICAN BEACH
DESTIN • FLORIDA

James F. Adams moved his family to Destin in 1981 from his hometown of Oxford, Miss. At that time, Destin was a "sleepy" village, with no fast food, grocery, or drug store chains, and very few restaurants. He had come to Destin to pursue a real estate opportunity, with plans to stay one year. Now, 22 years later, his legacy of development includes numerous town homes, The Neighborhood of Caribe, and four beach towers along the Gulf, the most exciting of which are Pelican Beach Resort and The Terrace, known as "The Resorts of Pelican Beach." This beautiful resort complex, whose name was inspired by fellow Mississippian John Grisham's thriller

"The Pelican Brief," hosts thousands of vacationers each year. The inspiration for its logo (a pelican riding on the back of a dolphin swimming) was a passage Jim read in Waller's "The Bridges of Madison County." From a small duplex town home in 1981 to this high-rise paradise, Jim's life has taken a "full turn." He and his family still love Destin, its casual lifestyle, and the many friends they have made there over the years, and they are recognized as being an important part of Destin's economic success.

"The Resorts of Pelican Beach" is Destin's favorite vacation condominium rental. It has added a new level of style and hospitality in the heart of Destin, providing relaxed elegance with a total amenity package. Overlooking the world-famous white sandy beaches, accommodations offer spectacular views of the Gulf, "Terrace Lake" and the Destin Harbor. Guests enjoy three adult pools with beautiful views, while children splash in their own kiddie pool. There are conference-meeting facilities, a poolside deli for snacks and a beachfront tiki bar for frozen drinks. Tennis courts, video game rooms, two spas, and a children's recreation room—the Pelican's Playzone—provide guests of all ages with endless activities. One, two, and three-bedroom accommodations have everything you need for a comfortable and relaxing stay. The Resorts of Pelican Beach can help make your visit to Destin a truly unforgettable experience. For more information, call toll free 888-735-4226, 850-654-1425 or visit www.pelican-beach.com online. *(Featured on the front cover and in front section of the book.)*

DALE E PETERSON VACATIONS

Destin is pure delight! With its magnificent white beaches and startling clear water, it is no surprise that it has been voted one of the top family vacation resorts in America. It's everything a vacation spot could possibly be, and through the years, families have come to depend on Dale E. Peterson Vacations to provide them with the perfect place to enjoy all that Destin has to offer. Well-known and respected in the area as one of Destin's premiere vacation rentals, it offers accommodations, including: high-rise condominiums, cozy cottages, or sunny beach houses. Whether you need a two-story penthouse condominium or a studio apartment, Dale E. Peterson Vacations can help. The friendly, professional agents will assist you in either purchasing a permanent home or finding the perfect vacation summer rental. They know the area and all its offerings. Their properties are near top-ranked golf courses; wonderful shopping districts; antique malls; and Destin Harbor. Visit Monday-Saturday 8:30 am-5 pm daily at 321 Hwy. 98 E., or call 850-654-4747, 800-336-9669 or for more information, visit www.destinresorts.com.

THE ISLANDER
CONDOMINIUM ASSOCIATION

They have been doing it right at The Islander for more than 20 years. Two generations of families have been coming to The Islander Condominium for days in the sun and a lifetime of memories. Located at 502 Gulf Shore Dr. on Holiday Isle near popular Destin restaurants and attractions, The Islander is a family-oriented beach resort featuring two-bedroom/two-bath units with a beautiful gulf view; two lighted tennis courts; two heated swimming pools; two whirlpools; barbeque grills; and sailboats. And that's everything you need for a perfect Destin vacation! For more information, call 800-477-8837, 850-837-1000 or visit www.islander-resort.com. Be an Islander!

If you could imagine the "picture perfect" vacation, it would be here, at the Silver Shells Beach Resort & Spa, 15000 Emerald Coast Pkwy. The stretch of emerald green water against the silver-white sands of Destin is the setting for this incredible resort and spa. Sprawling across 31-acres, with 1,100 feet of private beachfront and luxurious residences, Destin's newest and most upscale resort offers complimentary beach service; poolside cabanas; a beachside bar and grill; hot tubs; watersport rentals; and organized beach activities. Whether you choose to lounge on the pristine beach; float your cares away in the beautiful pool; or simply enjoy the beauty of sailboats gliding across a burnt orange sunset; every minute of your stay will be unforgettable. Call Resort Property Management at 877-447-3767 or 850-650-9998. For a visual tour of the resort, visit www.DestinsBestRentals.com online.
(Color picture featured in front section of the book.)

Centrally located in the heart of Destin on Holiday Isle, the Inlet Reef Club, 506 Gulf Shore Dr., is perfect for a romantic escape for two, or a lively vacation for the entire family. Large two-and-three-bedroom condominium units feature sliding glass doors off the master and living areas, opening to the breath-taking views of the Gulf of Mexico. Guests have access to a beautiful, heated swimming pool; sauna; hot tub; and tennis court. And, the beach access is private. The staff is extremely friendly and accommodating, ensuring that your visit will be everything you could hope for and more. Call 850-837-2767, 800-367-1801 or visit www.inletreefclub.com.

Finding the perfect swimsuit is EASY, once you've found the perfect store. That perfect store is Sporty Lady, 4427 Commons Dr. E. in Destin in the Shoppes at Paradise Key. The hallmark of the store is its wonderful personal service. With more than 25 years in the swimwear business, the knowledgeable sales associates take pride in their ability to help each customer find a suit that maximizes her assets and minimizes her figure flaws. When a woman leaves Sporty Lady, she does so with confidence, knowing she has found a swimsuit that both fits and flatters. Many of their customers come to Sporty Lady for hard-to-find specialty suits such as mastectomy, maternity, long-torso, and bra-sized swimwear. Sporty Lady also carries numerous groups of mix and match separates with tops from AA-EE and bottoms from 4-18. There are more than 10,000 suits from more than 50 manufacturers from here and abroad—a diverse inventory of Missy, Junior and Girls' sizes, as well as Plus-sizes to size 32W.

Sporty ladies will also find the very latest in casual resortwear and unique sportswear, including coordinating jewelry, shoes, hats and bags. You'll love being able to customize and build your own outfit to suit your taste. Choose from popular cabana pants, tank dresses, halters, and pareos in no-wrinkle fabrics that take the worry out of looking great! Whether you need a new bathing suit for a pool party, or an entire sporty wardrobe for an upcoming vacation—Sporty Lady has got you covered.

Store hours are seasonal so please call 850-837-6763 for more information or visit www.sportylady.com on-line.

Jim Ball, Inc.
BOUTIQUES

"Whatever Your Style, We Have Your Store!" This slogan sums up the commitment and mission of the Jim Ball, Inc. Boutiques of Florida. Rather than opening the same store in different places, they have opened different stores in the same place, and have received awards from *Emerald Coast Magazine* as "Best Local Retailer Overall," "Best Gift Store," "Best Men's Clothing Store," and "Best Woman's Clothing Store."

Founder Jim Ball opened his first store in Pensacola in 1974. In 1976, another store was opened in Santa Rosa Mall, Fort Walton Beach, and in 1985 a third was opened in its current location, 922 Hwy. 98 E. in Shoreline Mall, Destin. Jim Ball, Inc. currently consists of 15 stores from Orange Beach, Ala. to Carillon Beach, Fla.

Some of the wonderful stores within the Jim Ball, Inc. Boutiques include: Diva ("Glam" party and cocktail attire); Black n White Store (every woman's basics–black, white–always right); The Jean Store (great jeans and clothing to go with denim); Hepburn's (clothing for the timeless look in casual wear); Gidget's (beach brights and prints with the motif of careless fun and freedom); The Buzz (coolest store ever, with shoes, cosmetics, gifts, and home décor); and Tooley Home (Accoutrements For Living–home accent selections of gifts, furniture, books, gourmet food & coffee, art work, pillows, and candles).

Be sure to visit www.jimballinc.com online for an overview of all of the wonderful stores and their locations or call 850-837-1272, extension 209.

Cute name, cute owner, cute clothes! We loved every single thing about this wonderful and very popular clothing boutique at 34904 Emerald Coast Pkwy. in Destin. Owner Cheryl Chamblee who is one of the most energetic and enthusiastic people you will meet, had visited Destin for many years before deciding to stay and open a business.

In Girl Friend'z, she carries fashionable and "snappy" clothing for the young at heart—clothes that women enjoy to wear, and that give them a very definable style. Cheryl knows that women love to shop (whether they buy or not) in an environment that makes them feel comfortable, no matter their age. She tries very hard to make each customer feel special, finding the perfect clothing for her size, shape, and style. The store has become almost a "hang out" for her customers. Stop by once, and you'll understand why. Girl Friend'z is open Monday-Saturday 10 am-7 pm, Sunday noon-6 pm. We told you that Cheryl was energetic—she also owns a darling children's shop called Brat'z in the same shopping mall. Call 850-650-5477 for more information.

Barefoot Princess
A LILLY PULITZER® SIGNATURE STORE

What do you wear in paradise? How can you dress for a turquoise ocean and sugar white beaches? The answer is *Lilly Pulitzer®*! It's a Palm Beach thing. It offers the best selection in resort apparel. The collection includes merchandise for ladies, men, children and home; as well as ladies shoes, jewelry and accessories. Barefoot princess, located in the Market Shops at Sandestin, is open daily 10 am-6 pm off-season and 10 am-9 pm in-season. Visit www.sandestin.com or call 850-267-8179.

BOUTIQUE

For 15 years, Capapie's Boutique at 13330 W. Emerald Coast Pkwy. in Destin has been a favorite shopping destination for discriminating women looking for upscale resort wear. Hand-crafted jewelry, designer shoes, trendy bags, and darling hats complete special occasion ensembles from outrageous prom to sophisticated mother-of-the-bride.

Owner Gayle Warrick promises to dress you from "head to toe," which is what the word "Capapie" literally means. She and her staff are extremely courteous and helpful. Gayle's motto is…For all the best moments in your life, we give you clothes to live in…She has also recently added adorable play clothes for toddler boys and girls, as well as gifts for the home. Capapie's is open Monday-Saturday 10 am-5 pm. Call 850-654-9336.*(Color picture featured in front section of the book.)*

Love to shop? Then Sandestin Clothing Company, 9375 Emerald Coast Pkwy. W., in the Market Shops at Sandestin is for you. This wonderful shop carries lovely resort wear, beachwear and accessories—many featuring the Sandestin logo—as well as, Fresh Produce Sportswear. Stop by! The shop is open 10 am-9 pm during spring and summer, until 6 pm during fall and winter and Sunday 10 am-6 pm year round. Call 850-267-5550 or visit www.sandestin.com online.

SUNSET BIRKENSTOCK SHOES

If you're planning on lots of walking on your vacation, you may want to stop by Sunset Birkenstock Shoes first! This "one-stop shop" carries every good quality European comfort shoe sold in the United States—from Birkenstock's German sandals and shoes to Mephisto's European-made walking shoes.

Owned and operated by father-daughter team Eddy and Joy Hardy, Sunset Birkenstock Shoes is known for its customer service. Shipping is available anywhere in the United States, making it convenient for out-of-towners who can't find this unique footwear in their area.

Located at 9375 Hwy. 98 W. in The Market Shops at Sandestin, Sunset Birkenstock Shoes is open Monday-Saturday 10 am-9 pm and Sunday 10 am-6 pm. For more information, call 850-837-5466 or visit www.sunsetbirkenstock.com online.

FINE LADIES CLOTHIER

Sandstone Fine Ladies Clothier in the Fountain Plaza in Destin, offers women of the Emerald Coast exquisite clothes and fashion accessories from around the world. Owner Denise Mohylsky, continues to garner the admiration from others in her profession. With her finger on the pulse of the fashion world, Denise strives to find unusual, yet classic clothing that will be good investment pieces for her customers. As trends come and go, she has a talent for choosing clothes that hold their value. Sandstone is featured on national T.V.'s The Learning Channel's (TLC) "Make Over Story." She carries lines by wonderful designers such as Madeline Cranfill with Marisa Baratelli, and couture by Lili Butler, with accessories that will compliment any style. Sandstone, 12671 Hwy. 98 W., is also the perfect place to shop for beautiful "mother-of-the-bride," and eveningwear. The shop is open Monday-Saturday 10 am-6 pm. Call 850-654-1229.

Amy Cain has always been a shoe fanatic and wondered why there wasn't a shoe boutique in the Destin area that catered to a more unique, sophisticated taste. Motivated by this lack of venue, she took her love of shoes and opened up Shoo Fly Shoo.

Found at 34904 Emerald Coast Pkwy. Suite 122, this store's name isn't the only thing that makes it unique—Shoo Fly Shoo is not only a customer friendly store, but also a pet friendly store! Mingle with Amy and her pets as you browse through Destin's only selection of such designers as Hollywould, Carlos Santana, Rafé, Lily Holt and matching footwear and handbags by Icon and Cynthia Rowley.

This exclusive, high-end shoe boutique offers so much more than just the latest footwear. For an unforgettable shopping spree at Destin's finest, put Shoo Fly Shoo on you list of "musts"—and don't forget to bring along your favorite furry friend. Open Monday-Saturday 10 am-6 pm. For more information, call 850-650-7463.

Azure   BLUE MARLIN

For casual, comfy resort wear for men that inspires "fun in the sun" and "looking good," visit Azure/Blue Marlin at the Market Shops at Sandestin. This store has been a great hit with men, with lines like Nat Nast, Tommy Bahama and Tori Richard. Just so you'll be "in the know," the bowling shirt is back in a big way—you'll find them here! Browse, have fun and come back! Open Monday-Saturday 10 am-9 pm and Sunday until 6 pm, off season daily 10 am-6 pm. Call 850-837-1297.

Kiki Risa

Kiki Risa is a boutique, which stands alone for its unique clothing and accessories. It is Destin's most fashion-forward women's store to shop. The young and energetic owner and staff are eager to dress you in some of the newest and hottest lines, such as Theory, Trina Turk, Tibi, Susana Monaco and Paper Denim. Stop by 4421 Commons Dr. E. #B108 in Destin, and see for yourself. Kiki Risa is open Monday-Saturday 10 am-6 pm or call 850-650-0554.

IVY & IRIS

Plan early to book the flower-designing duo of Ann Wallace and Nancy Krenkel for your special occasion. They are much in demand, and they limit their jobs. Ann and Nancy are the talent behind Ivy and Iris, 244 Mattie's Way in Destin. When retirement approached for these dynamic women, they planned their "next career" together —only this time, doing something they truly loved. They design and fashion fresh flower bouquets and arrangements for weddings and special occasions. From start to finish, you'll love their work. References and portfolio viewing are available upon request. For appointment or information, call 850-837-9250 or 850-837-7061.

Mother, Father, three sons, two daughters, and a cousin—the entire family works together in this wonderful garden and gift store at 9755 Hwy. 98 W. in Destin. Potager's, known for its unique French, Italian, and Portuguese pottery, is a beautiful shop filled with wonderful things that will transform your home, patio, or garden. John and Patti Williams moved their close-knit family to Destin from Dallas, six years ago, so that they could enjoy life at a slower pace in their favorite vacation place. The furniture and home décor are timeless

pieces; things that will surely become treasured heirlooms and, the garden designs will add charm to your safe haven. The Williams say that they only sell things they absolutely love! We loved the exquisite bed linens and toiletries from Europe. Open 8 am-5 pm Monday-Saturday and 11 am-4 pm Sunday. For more information, call 850-269-3211 or visit www.potagers.net.

Gifts, Home Décor & Furniture

DESIGNER LAMPS AND SHADES

Light up your home or office with beautiful lamps and accessories from Designer Lamps and Shades, 36254 Emerald Coast Pkwy. Owned and operated by the entire Kidwell family since 1989, this gorgeous lighting showroom features more than 1,200 wall, floor, and table lamps, as well as chandeliers, and palm fans from manufacturers such as Waterford, Sedgefield, Frederick Cooper, Wildwood, Maitland-Smith and Fine Art.

Designer Lamps and Shades carries 1,500 different lampshades, from designer silks to hard back, and offers shade recovery and lamp repair. Add a beautiful, decorative, and very popular finial or tassel to your lamps for a festive touch. Along with the beautiful lighting, you'll find accent furniture, decorative mirrors in every size, framed artwork, and beautiful floral designs. You can't beat these adorable accessories. The showroom is gorgeous, and the owners are genuinely warm and welcoming. Hours are Monday-Friday 9 am-5 pm and Saturday until 4:30 pm. Call 850-837-3736 for more information.

Needa's This & Thats

Upon entering Needa's This & Thats you'll notice a reflection of timeless elegance. Venita Brannon, known by all as Needa, opened her store in 1996 at 13370 W. Emerald Coast Pkwy. in Destin, fulfilling a long-time dream. She had been designing gift baskets from her husband's office for years, and had such a following, that it was a natural step to open her own special place.

She has ingeniously blended the old with the new, providing exquisite antiques and an assortment of unique gift items and home accessories. Because Needa had also been a wedding coordinator for many years, she carries the finest china patterns with a broad variety of bridal registry goodies. You can select from the finest designs of personal stationery and bridal invitations from William Arthur and Crane, as well as social invitations, that she can print in-house.

A complimentary custom gift-wrap is a signature that keeps customers coming back. You'll love being able to stop in at the last minute, pick up a wonderful gift, and leave with it beautifully wrapped on the way to the party! If you can't stop in, your gift selection is just a call away. Her fabulous gift baskets for every occasion can be delivered by UPS upon request. Also, be sure to ask Needa about her line of skin care products and make-up formulated in Switzerland. You'll love meeting Needa, she is an enthusiastic, talented woman who loves her customers. Needa's This & Thats is open Monday-Saturday 10 am-5 pm. For more information, call 850-837-5998.

RESORT INTERIORS

Julie and Frank Kovach challenge you to "expect something different" at the largest home furnishings showroom and design center on the Emerald Coast. This exceptional design center contains more than 28,000 sq. ft. Exclusive furniture lines, rugs, art, lamps and accessories from around the world are displayed in model rooms. You'll find the latest Hemingway, Tommy Bahama, and Henredon Gallery selections, as well as stylish pieces from Lane, Bernhardt, and Stanley. Expert designers and decorators will help you choose everything from floor coverings to wall hangings, creating your dream home. This "one source shopping" concept has helped make Resort Interiors at 11224 Emerald Coast Pkwy. in Destin the third fastest growing company and the "Top Retailer" in the state of Florida. Hours are Monday-Friday 9 am-5 pm and Saturday 10 am-5 pm. Visit www.resortinteriors.com or call 888-837-6886, 850-837-6886.

Trim, tassels, bead fringes, tiebacks, braids, and oh yes, ostrich feather trim! We've found the most adorable fabric and accessory shop that carries all of these very popular, yet hard to find fabric adornments. Cover Stories is the culmination of a realized dream for Martha McDonald (mom) and Jennifer Stennett (daughter). The darling designing duo began sewing for people in their "garage workroom" until the little yellow house at 174 Azalea Dr. in Destin became available. Inside you'll find many bolts of fabric in stock including beautiful silks, linens, tapestries and chenilles, and literally thousands of samples from vendors like Waverly, Fabricut, and Duralee. Cover Stories is open Monday-Friday 9:30 am-5 pm, Saturday by appointment. Call 850-654-3060.

THE FINEST
CONSIGNMENT FURNITURE, Inc.

Sherry Miller moved to Destin from New Jersey in 1978 as a single mom with three kids and a lot of determination. She has remained here these past 25 years, become completely immersed in the community, and is now the owner of several furniture consignment shops with sons Justin and Samuel. The Destin store is located at 707 Hwy. 98 E., #1, with others in Pensacola and Gulf Breeze. She came up with the idea for furniture consignment as she watched people constantly remodeling and updating resorts. "If clothing consignment worked so successfully, why not furniture?" she thought. Sherry only accepts quality pieces she would have in her own home, and prices items very reasonably. Destin locals have come to depend on Sherry's ability to turn her inventory quickly, and love finding one-of-a-kind pieces for themselves. Hours are Monday-Saturday 9 am-5 pm and Sunday noon-5 pm. Call 850-654-5995.

Meg Jones got all she ever wanted when her husband Whip bought her a small gift shop in The Market Shops at Sandestin one Christmas. It is called "My Favorite Things," and is filled with our favorite things like the exquisite Vietri line of imported, hand-painted pottery; collectible porcelain animals by Herend; Arthur Court; Vera Bradley; and the very collectible Swarovski Crystal. Visit My Favorite Things at 9375 Hwy. 98 W., #10, daily 10 am-6 pm. Call 850-269-2611.

Infinity FLOORING
· Carpet · Tile · Wood · Area Rugs

Whether your home needs a durable, sensible floor at a competitive price, or a stunning, custom application to exceed even your expectations, Infinity Flooring is a store that combines all of your floor covering needs in one simple solution. The expansive showroom located at 296 S. Holiday Rd. between Emerald Coast Pkwy. and Scenic Gulf Dr. in Destin, showcases a large selection of carpeting; area rugs; pre-engineered woods; cork; ceramic tile; porcelain tile; and natural stone; as well as innovative new products including leather flooring.

Infinity Flooring is a descendant of Carpet Clearance Warehouse, which originated in 1984 in Colorado with Buffalo Bob's and Mad Man Mark's very successful commercials. Owner/Manager Leisa Johnson (Buffalo Bob's daughter and partner) says, "I love helping homeowners with all facets of choosing their floor coverings."

The professional staff is friendly and knowledgeable, but not intrusive. The showroom is open Monday-Friday 9 am-5 pm and Saturday, by appointment only. Call 850-650-1039 or visit www.infinityfloors.com.

Gourmet, Specialty Foods & Wines

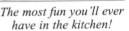

The most fun you'll ever have in the kitchen!

When you walk through the doors of Kitchenique at The Market Shops at Sandestin, you know immediately that you are in for a fun and *delicious* treat! Kitchenique is so appropriately named because it is truly the most unique kitchen store imaginable. Since 1985, Kitchenique has carried all the latest gadgets, cookbooks, gourmet coffees, teas and foods, as well as the highest quality cookware, bakeware and cutlery. Walk toward the kitchen, and you will be invited to taste the day's samplings of gourmet foods. The friendly, well-trained staff is quick to make cooking suggestions; demonstrate anything from a gadget to a top-of-the-line espresso machine; or grab an item from the fridge for a taste test. On a regular basis, up to 22 cooking school students gather around the counter of the professionally-outfitted kitchen to sample dishes prepared by the area's most talented chefs, and enjoy wines paired to compliment each delicious meal. For a complete schedule of classes, visit www.kitchenique.com online. Located at 9375 Hwy 98 W., #7, Kitchenique is open Monday-Saturday 10 am-9 pm and Sunday until 6 pm during the summer months and Monday-Sunday 10 am-6 pm during the winter months. Call locally 850-837-0432 or toll-free 800-476-2918.

Named "Best Wine Shop" by the *Emerald Coast Magazine,* and "Best Wine Selection" by *Independent Florida Sun Newspaper,* Chan's Wine World at 4424 Commons Dr. in Destin, has been called an "Adult Toys-R-Us." Its world-class, value priced wines, gift baskets, and wine accessories have made Chan's the must see wine shop of Northwest Florida. Equally impressive is the extensive selection of single malt scotches, aged rums and tequilas, imported vodkas and single barrel bourbons, and more than 150 beers. With two Certified Wine Educators on staff, they can help you find the right wine or spirit for dinner tonight or a large party. For a special night, attend one of Chan's Wine Tastings every Friday 5-7 pm. For information or to sign up for the monthly newsletter, call 850-269-2909. Open 9 am-9 pm Monday-Thursday, 9 am-10 pm Friday-Saturday and 1-9 pm on Sunday.

(Vin'tij) Wine Boutique

Market • Bar • Bistro

Combine just the right amount of food, a fun atmosphere, and lots of wine, and you will have discovered (Vintij) Wine Boutique & Bistro at 10859 Emerald Coast Pkwy., Suite 103 in Destin. Todd and Sabrina Reber and Chef John Jacob opened this unique wine boutique in 1998, and it was an instant hit. It received "Restaurant of the Year" in 2000 and in 2002; was named one of *Florida Trend Magazine's* Top 400 Restaurants; and garnered the very prestigious "Wine Spectator Award of Excellence." The award-winning menu is ever-changing, and tantalizing, focusing on fresh local flavors, and including items like John's Oyster BLT and Roast Garlic Seared Yellow Fin Tuna. You'll love the enormous selection of hand-picked boutique wines, wine accessories, and gift baskets, along with the informative wine tastings on Thursdays. Hours are 11 am-12 am daily. Call 850-650-9820 or visit www.vintij.com.

Interior Design

Lovelace Interiors is the most widely published and nationally recognized interior design firm on the Emerald Coast. Since 1991, Lovelace Interiors at 12870 U.S. Hwy. 98 W. in Destin has built a reputation as the premiere design and home accents store in the Southeast. It has been featured in Architectural Digest, Florida Design, Coastal Living and Veranda Magazine. International awards such as the ARTS Award and regional awards such as the "Best of The Emerald Coast" are a sign of the designer's commitment to their clients and profession. The Watercolor showroom showcases southern coastal—low country style indicative of the original Florida cottages on the Gulf Coast.

The Destin showroom continues to specialize in a mixture of graceful, elegant styles. Stop by their constantly changing showrooms and experience "The Art of Design." Call 850-837-5563.

The designers at Coastal Design Studio, 8955 Hwy. 98 W., Suite 106 in Destin, offer custom interior design services. With years of experience from the expert talents of Georgia Carlee, Vickie Coit, Marlene Freeman, Suzanne Harman, Kelly Porter Smith, and Leigh Wright. Their extensive resource library includes a unique variety of furnishings, fabrics, wallcoverings and window treatments to complete any design project! Call 850-622-2380 for an appointment.

INTERIOR DESIGN STUDIO

The designers at Killough's Interior Design Studio, 501A Hwy. 98 E., are not only very talented, but also intuitive in their creativity. Maybe that's why Killough's is known as one of Destin's top design centers. Owners Gary Killough and David Parello not only frequent the major American markets, but also travel internationally to bring beautiful and enduring items to complement their clients' homes, gardens, yachts and condominiums surpassing their clients' expectations. You'll appreciate the one-stop shopping destination for furniture, lamps, artwork, and more. The merchandise is displayed in beautifully designed vignettes, allowing customers a glimpse into the designers' ideas. Hours are Monday-Friday 9 am-5 pm and Saturday 10 am-4 pm. Call 850-654-5006.

DUCE & COMPANY

Duce & Company is a full-service interior design firm showcasing fine furniture, accessories, art and textiles. Duce & Company designers create spectacular interiors for the most discriminating clients. If you are traditional, cutting-edge, beach casual, or elegantly formal, they can meet your needs. Services include: design concepts, budget consultation, space planning, and project management. The company targets high-end residential, hospitality and commercial interiors. The Duce & Company showroom is located at 12381-A Emerald Coast Pkwy. in Destin. Open Monday-Friday 10 am-6 pm and Saturday 10 am-5 pm. Call 850-654-7490. *(Color picture featured in front section of the book.)*

MCCASKILL & COMPANY
— Finest Jewelry & Watches —

McCaskill & Company is the realization of a childhood dream for jeweler Bill Campbell. As a young boy who had a special relationship with his grandmother, Gussie McCaskill Campbell, Bill spent many pleasurable hours with her in a fantasyland of beautiful precious jewels, which her father had brought home from travels all over the world. Bill's fascination and love for jewelry never waned through 20 years of working in the family hardware business. Now, as a jeweler, he brings to his clientele an expertise born not only of knowledge, but also of a true love for his work. Since its inception eight years ago, McCaskill & Company has earned the reputation as the areas most distinctive couture jewelry gallery along the Emerald Coast. McCaskill & Company takes pride in being able to showcase the finest jewels and watches which include: Henry Dunay, Chopard, Louis Glick, Oscar Heyman & Brothers, Ambar, Paul Morelli, Steven Lagos John Hardy and more. Bill and Elizabeth Campbell invite you to McCaskill & Company at 13390 Hwy. 98 W. in Destin to *"Experience the Difference."* Call 850-650-2262, or visit www.mccaskillcompany.com. *(Color picture featured in front section of the book.)*

Destin Jewelers

Awarded "Best Jewelry Store" by *Emerald Coast Magazine*, Destin Jewelers has been recognized for its customer service and unique designs. Shop in Destin at 14091-B Emerald Coast Pkwy., Monday-Saturday 9:30 am-5:30 pm (850-837-8822), or in Sandestin at 144 Fisherman's Cove located in the Village of Baytowne Wharf, daily 10 am-9 pm (850-622-0984). Or, visit www.destinjewelers.com. *(See back cover.)*

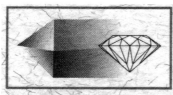

HDS DIAMONDS

Dany Robertson is one of the most honest and likeable businessmen you will ever meet. And, HDS Diamonds is an exceptional jewelry brokerage and appraisal service specializing in fine diamonds; colored stones; pearls; fine watches; gold; and platinum jewelry. His stellar reputation and longevity in the jewlery business has made HDS Diamonds one of Destin's best jewelry businesses. For appointment, call 850-654-3919 or e-mail drobertson507@earthlink.net online.

*Ever stop to think and
then forget to start again?*
—Unknown

This "Gourmutt Bakery" is for the dogs! Literally! The Doggy Bag pet bakery at 34904 Emerald Coast Pkwy., # 126, is a fun, unique bakery where your pet can sample delicious bakery items. They'll look good enough that you'll be tempted to munch, too, but don't. This fine food is just for Fido. Treats baked daily include tasty carob-drenched cookies; yogurt dipped treats; "pupcakes;" bagels; and even doggie birthday cakes. Owners Bill and Jodi Ketchersid loved visiting a pet bakery in Miami, but after moving to Destin, realized there was nothing like it anywhere in the area. Their two big retrievers are soooo happy that their owners have opened this special bakery, because they are the built-in quality-control tasters! In addition to quality food and treats, and specialty bakery items, you'll also find a large selection of pet bedding; collars; leashes; bath products; and even doggie nail polish! The bakery is open Monday-Saturday 10 am-7 pm and Sunday 1-5 pm, or you may shop at www.destindoggybag.com online. Call 850-837-9833.

VILLAGE GROOMER, INC.

Four-legged friends of all sizes and shapes love it when their families vacation in Destin. That's because they get to stay with Penny Vance and staff at Village Groomer, 211-1 Main St. Specializing in precision grooming for all canine breeds, Penny has a reputation for being one of the best groomers in the area. Her sweet, caring way with animals has made Village Groomer a favorite place for grooming and boarding for more than 17 years. Hours are Tuesday-Saturday 8 am-5:30 pm and Sunday-Monday 9-10 am for boarding pick-up and drop-off. Call 850-837-0455.

The staff at The Spa at Silver Shells invites you to relax your body . . . clear your mind . . . and renew your spirit, with an array of disciplines including aroma therapy; massage therapy; hydrotherapy; and skin, hair, and nail care. All of the services are provided for both men and women (yes, "real men" do spas) in the comfort of private treatment rooms, and all of the products are marine and/or plant based. Clinical skin care includes micro-dermabrasion (called the "lunch time" face peel), Lam Probe, and Lymphobiology. Be sure to ask about the Deluxe French Body Polish—an invigorating exfoliation treatment that gently polishes away dry, dull skin. Enjoy the benefits of an outdoor swimming pool, saunas, steam rooms, whirlpools, and a co-ed fitness center. Stop by The Spa at 15000 Emerald Coast Pkwy. in Destin. For reservations, call 850-337-5107 or visit www.thespaatsilvershells.com online. *(Color picture featured in front section of the book.)*

Deborah Vizzina is a make-up artist with many years of experience with a national cosmetic company. Her expertise has made The Change Salon at The Plaza, 4507 Furling Ln., # 109, one of the most respected salons in Destin. The seven hair and color specialists and two nail specialists are some of the best in the business. Deborah is a very talented owner who loves helping people look and feel beautiful! Open Monday-Friday 8 am-8 pm and Saturday until 5 pm. Call 850-650-6444.

ANGIE'S NAILS

Simply put—Angie Fagan is dedicated. She says, "I care about the health as much as the look." Her "no drilling" technique and 18 years experience offer you "the" most natural look in acrylics—specializing in pink and whites. Angie is a native, a mother-of-two and a local favorite. She's located inside The Master's Touch Salon at 12889 Emerald Coast Pkwy., #103, at the Miramar Plaza in Destin. Open Monday-Friday 10 am-5 pm. Call 850-650-1670.

Destin MedSpa

Anti-Aging & Wellness Center

Destin MedSpa is the perfect place to relax, renew, and rejuvenate while being pampered to perfection. Located at 36008 Emerald Coast Pkwy., two blocks east of Destin Commons, Destin MedSpa offers "Clinical Anti-Aging in a Relaxed Atmosphere." Owner Lenny Arendt and brothers Keith and Kent have been in the anti-aging and cosmetic laser industries since 1992. The Dermaglide® microdermabrasion system pioneered by them is the first to use organic baking soda crystals. It comfortably removes sun damage, acne scars and blemishes. The exclusive Eye-Touch® process tightens and rejuvenates the most delicate of tissues—Eyelids. "Looking good now feels great!" Professional massage services are also available.

"Beautiful Skin is Always In!"® Anti-Aging Parties with "The Works" are exciting at Destin MedSpa, or at your place. Destin MedSpa can help you look and feel your absolute best before those very special occasions. Gift certificates and a wide variety of personal care products are available. Demonstrations and consultation are complimentary. Stop by Tuesday-Saturday 10 am-6 pm (other hours by appointment). Call 850-837-3334 or 1-888-SPA-GLOW.

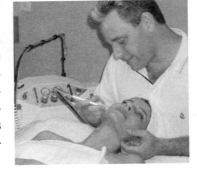

Like the famous Palais Versailles, which calls forth sumptuous images of "living well," the artisans of Versailles invite you to enjoy their version of the ultimate in indulgence at the beautiful Versailles of Destin.

The arched stone building at 10123 US Hwy. 98 W., is filled with beautiful furnishings, soft music, and caring people who want one thing—to make you look and feel fabulous!

Spa services include restorative and clinical skincare; spa facials; specialty waxing and electrolysis; "hairchitecture;" nail sculpting; as well as other fine spa services. Expert estheticians offer microdermabrasion, chemical peels, and more. The spa is open Tuesday-Saturday 9 am-5 pm, or for special appointments, call 850-650-8095.

SIMPLE PLEASURES

From an early age, Yvette Nation discovered the value of indulging in one of life's most wonderful simple pleasures—the bubble bath. In her cozy shop she features special soaps, makeup and fragrances from around the world; delicious candles; air scents; and even laundry soap that is "rumored" to make doing the laundry more fun! Discover life's "simple pleasures" at 10123 U.S. Hwy. 98 W in Destin. Open 9 am - 5 pm Tuesday-Saturday. Call 850-650-3004.

DESTIN ICE SEAFOOD MARKET & DELI

When Dwane Martin retired during the 1980s, he decided to move to Destin, and happened upon the Destin Ice House, that was for sale. He purchased it in 1985 and definitely found himself out of retirement! Local boat captains began asking him to buy their seafood, and a whole new part of the business was born. Destin Ice Seafood Market & Deli is located at 663 Hwy. 98 in a quaint red-shuttered "barn," and is open daily from 8 am-6 pm. Customers stand in line for the top-quality specialty meats and seafood. You'll also find a great selection of gourmet grocery items and fine wines. Some of Dwane's most popular items are the specialty foods like the Turducken—a boneless chicken, stuffed into a boneless duck, stuffed into a boneless turkey! He says that these are fast replacing the traditional baked ham or roasted turkey for holiday dinners. Another local favorite is the selection of delicious fresh seafood salads served daily. The service is excellent; the products fresh and top-quality; and the atmosphere very authentic Destin. Call 850-837-8333.

Specialty Shops

This adorable fine stationery and monogramming store is as fun as its name—Hooch & Holly's—which, by the way, are the names of the furry bunnies that live in the store to welcome and delight visitors. Owners Candace Abuvala and Shelley Scholl have created a store specializing in the rare and stunning "never seen before" collections of invitations; announcements; and stationery. In addition, they offer a wide selection of gifts for babies, weddings, birthdays, or our favorite—girlfriends! For the beautiful Emerald Coast brides, there is a full-service beach wedding consultation for programs, invitations, bridal stationery, wedding albums, guestbooks, bridesmaids and groomsmen gifts.

Hooch & Holly's is located at 36132 Emerald Coast Pkwy., Suite 2 in Destin, 1 mile east of the Mid-Bay Bridge and is open Monday through Saturday 10 am-5 pm. Call 850-837-1960.

Tis the Season

CHRISTMAS & GIFTS

The Market Shops at Sandestin

Christmas fairy tales do come true, and not just in places covered with snow! For Curt and Jennifer Weintraub, owners of Tis the Season, their "fairy-land" is warm, and one filled with joy all year.

Tis the Season is located at 9375 Emerald Coast Pkwy. in Destin and is open daily 10 am-9 pm during summer and until 6 pm in the winter.

The Weintraubs purchased the store from two sisters and their friend who started it more than 20 years ago. In carrying on this incredible tradition, Curt and Jennifer provide only the highest quality Christmas merchandise. From traditional Christmas items like Clothtique Santas and Byers' Choice Carolers to unique seaside Christmas decorations—you'll find utterly fabulous treasures to add to your Christmas wonderland! Enjoy the festive music and the sparkling lights of Tis the Season. Visit www.tistheseason.net or call 850-837-9730.

Art and glass are brilliantly fused together in this unique gallery that serves as Destin's first bead shop. Art~itude boasts a selection of more than 2,000 styles for the bead enthusiast. Lampwork, polymer clay, and fused glass beads are among a few of the specialty beads. You'll also find a vast selection of Czech glass, Swarovski crystals, delicas, tohos, shell and bone beads. On-site classes include stringing, beadweaving, and wire-working. See the class schedule at www.artitudebeads.com.

Barbara Marie's designs are all created with Art~itude beads and are displayed among art glass pieces handcrafted by more than 20 American artists. Sun catchers, slumped bowls, blown marbles, and one-of-a-kind kaleidoscopes all cast their colorful charm throughout the gallery. Whether a bead enthusiast, a glass aficionado, or a lover of color and art, there's something for everyone at Art~itude Beads and Art Glass, located at 860 Hwy. 98 E., at Shoreline Mall in Destin. Open Monday-Saturday 10 am-8 pm during the summer and until 5:30 pm in the winter. Call 850-650-7791.

Be careful about reading health books.
You may die of a misprint.

—Mark Twain

Tearooms

Magnolia & Ivy

Antiques • Gifts • Tea Parlor

Enter the opulently decorated Magnolia & Ivy Tearoom in the Village of Baytowne Wharf in Sandestin, and you will feel as though you've been transported to the Queen of England's favorite tearoom, or perhaps Mariage Freres in Paris. With its highlights of gold accenting the ornate molding, and the ceiling painted to look like a sea-blue sky blushed by dawn, the tearoom affords a romantic, elegant, and very feminine ambiance for afternoon tea. This authentic Southern tearoom is housed off a New Orleans-style brick courtyard, complete with gas lights and French balconies. Here, afternoon tea is presented on three-tiered servers, including freshly-baked scones, homemade sweets, and beautiful finger sandwiches.

Owners Kay Snipes and Terri Eager opened their first Magnolia & Ivy tearoom in the small town of Parrott, Ga., before opening several more throughout the South. Their tearooms overflow with nostalgic touches such as vintage hats, dresses, gloves, and furs so little girls—and big girls too—can "play!" Tiny finger sandwiches are tied with ribbons, and delicate desserts are served on delicate china.

When the opportunity presented itself for a location at the Village of Baytowne Wharf, Terri and Kay decided to relocate their main business to Florida. A visit to the tearoom at 147 Market St. is an amazing experience. Whether you are "taking tea," or browsing the floor-to-ceiling displays of teapots, tea wares, books, Victorian knick-knacks, dishes, and silver—*you* will feel like a queen. The tearoom is open seven days a week 10 am-10 pm on-season and until 9 pm off-season. Call 850-267-2595 or visit www.magnoliaivy.com for reservations or information. The sisters invite you to, "Taste and see that the Lord is good." Psalms 34:8.

A woman is like a tea bag...
you don't know how strong she is
until you put her in hot water.

—Eleanor Roosevelt

DISCOVER APALACHICOLA

Though Florida has attracted tourists for decades, the Sunshine State still has a few well-hidden secrets tucked under its sprawling live oaks. Apalachicola is one of those gems. Its name, probably from the Hitchiti Indian language, means "those people on the other shore." With something for the antique lover, the nature lover, and the woman who just wants to slow down and enjoy its Southern charm, Apalachicola and the surrounding areas will sweep you into another era.

If you want to stroll by charming Victorian homes; peruse quaint antique shops; watch the sunset over the Gulf of Mexico; or relish the gentle sway of sea grasses on quiet beaches; you'll love this slice of heaven on Florida's panhandle. It will remind you of a time when neighbors enjoyed cold glasses of iced tea on the veranda, as well as strolling along tree-lined streets. In fact, 'Apalach", as it is sometimes called by the locals, has only one traffic light (and that's just a blinker!) So, come enjoy the secret that Florida has been saving just for you—and get swept away!

Then and Now

Apalachicola still maintains the quaint charm of its history as a small Southern port town. In the 1840s, Apalachicola was a thriving gateway to Europe and the West Indies. In fact, it was the second largest port in the state, with cotton as its primary shipment. As the railroad expanded, causing sea and river shipments to decrease, Apalachicola's commerce changed. Its tenants began milling the large cypress trees in the area, thus developing large lumber mills that ran into the late 1800s. That same lumber was responsible for the beautiful Victorian homes that are scattered throughout this lovely city. In fact, today, Apalachicola has more than 200 historical homes and buildings on the National Register.

By the end of the 1800s, Apalachicola's industry began to shift again, this time to fishing. Today, commercial fishing operations and a thriving art colony exist side by side, offering visitors the most delicious treats from the sea, as well as great shopping and beautiful museums. The Apalachicola of today has been described as "what Key West used to be, before it became Key West." It is a small, beautiful, friendly little fishing village filled with history, adventure, and friendly natives.

Exploring Nature

If your idea of a relaxing vacation includes casting your line into some of the best fishing—fresh water and salt water—in the country, then the Apalachicola Bay is where you want to be. Apalachicola is famous for some of the best oysters in the world. You will also find those who travel here to go "scalloping." "Scalloping" is an event, so be sure and ask one of the locals to give you the "scoop on scalloping." With varieties of fish like the spotted sea trout, the Spanish mackerel, oysters, scallops, and more, you'll find the perfect catch to fill your net. Several charter companies are available to help you locate the perfect spot to drop your line.

For more information on Apalachicola, contact the Apalachicola Chamber of Commerce at 850-653-9419 or visit www.apalachicolabay.org online.

Apalachicola
Fairs Festivals & Fun

February
   Annual Forgotten Coast's Chef Sampler

March
   Charity Chili Cook Off & Auction

April
   Historic Apalachicola Antique & Classic Boat Show

May
   Annual Spring Tour of Historic Homes

June
   Blue Parrot Annual Mullet Toss
   Big Bend Saltwater Classic Fishing Tournament

October
   Wildflower & Birding Festival

November
   Annual Florida Seafood Festival
   Historic Apalachicola Merchant's Assoc.Christmas Celebration

Attractions, Entertainment & Fishing

B-9 MARINE, INC.

Owner Larry Covell's family has been involved with the fishing industry for five generations. Whether you want to launch your boat at their ramp, or experience the fishing charter of a lifetime, B-9 Marine, Inc., 317 Water St. in Apalachicola, is the place. Captain Larry also offers Bay and Apalachicola River scenic tours; kayak rentals; and Eco-tours. Summer hours are Monday-Sunday 7 am-5 pm. Call 850-653-8860 or visit www.b9marine.com online.

Bed & Breakfasts, Inns & Rentals

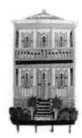

Wind - de - Mer Guesthouse

Wind-de-Mer Guesthouse is located in the heart of Apalachicola, one block off Hwy. 98 on 5th St., in Apalachicola's Historic Northside. Begin your vacation with complimentary wine and tapas served and enjoyed by both guests and resident owners Rob and Cathie Peterson.

The Guesthouse offers two spacious queen-sized suites both with private baths, and sitting areas with wonderful wrap-around porches. Bring your bike or enjoy a short two-block walk to the working riverfront, or downtown shopping, dining and entertainment. For those lazy days, relax with TV, complete with HBO and VCR in each room. A light-and-healthy breakfast is served by former chef Rob on the balcony or in the intimate dining room. The Wind-de-Mer Guesthouse motto: "Relax! This is your vacation!" For more information, visit www.floridaforgottencoast.com online or call 850-653-1675.

⚓ Anchor Realty & Mortgage Co.

Whether you're interested in a vacation rental or purchase, Anchor Realty and Mortgage Co. has quite a selection! Each house is unique from its décor to its wide variety of amenities such as full kitchens, Jacuzzis and even elevators.

With the one-of-a-kind Florida style architecture and the luxury of being close to the "white, sandy beaches," these houses stand out in beauty and view. One of the many benefits of Anchor is the solid return on its properties. Customers have received up to a 35 percent annual return on investments.

Besides offering some of the best deals and locations in town, Anchor Realty and Mortgage Co., with seven offices along the coast, offers something that even its Realtors can't put a price on— quality of life in a pristine environment.

For more information, call 850-653-3336 or 800-624-3964. Or visit www.florida-beach.com online.

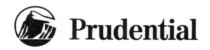

Resort Realty

Prudential Resort Realty, 123 W. Gulf Beach Dr., offers the largest selection of luxury beach vacation rental homes on St. George Island. The employees at Prudential go out of their way to make sure their guests find the perfect property that will make their vacation dreams a reality.

Vacationing on a barrier island with uncrowded white sand beaches and a bountiful bay offers families the opportunity to enjoy nature at its best; water sports, bird-watching, world-class fishing, stargazing or just plain relaxing. Best of all, many of the homes welcome your pet!

Prudential Resort Realty is open daily 9 am-5 pm. The friendly staff personifies "Southern hospitality." For more information or reservations, visit www.stgeorgeisland.com online or call them at 800-332-5196.

Books, Gifts & Home Décor

HOOKED ON BOOKS

At the center of downtown Apalachicola, next to one of the oldest buildings in town, you'll find this quaint little bookstore. Hooked on Books, 54 Market St., has books of all sorts. You will find books on Apalachicola History as well as wildlife guides for the area. We loved the wide assortment of cookbooks. The store is closed on Wednesday, but open the rest of the week from 10 am-5 pm and Sunday noon-5pm. Owner Judy Shultz also has a store in St. George Island, 116 E. Pine Ave. Call 850-653-2420.

Gadgets, gadgets, and more gadgets for the chef in you! You'll find every imaginable kitchen tool, glassware, cookware, bakeware, and barware at Rutabaga's, 73 Market St. in Apalachicola. Owner Carla Whitehead says her entire family helps make Rutabaga's one of the town's favorite places to shop. Customers call it "The Williams-Sonoma of Apalachicola." Be sure to take advantage of the wonderful Gift and Bridal Registry. Call 850-653-1101.

RIVERFRONT THERAPY

Kathy Jansen takes the idea of "therapy" to a new dimension. Riverfront Therapy at 313 Water St. #B5 in Apalachicola is literally "on the river." Kathy built the adorable Gingerbread-style, shingled cottage on pontoons. This creates a peaceful and comfortable massage experience while rocking with the rhythm of the water. A former professional dancer, Kathy uses her knowledge of the body to enhance her treatments. Enjoy hot stone massage, private yoga sessions, Reiki (energy work), and Cranio-Sacral Therapy®. Kathy also shares alternate healthcare ideas by bringing in other teachers for workshops such as partner massage, philosophy, and nutrition. Kathy is in-tune with the special needs of each client. For more information, visit www.riverfronttherapy.com or call 850-899-1079.

DISCOVER
CARILLON BEACH /
ROSEMARY BEACH /
SEAGROVE BEACH

These peaceful beaches stretch along Florida's panhandle, masterfully melding man's blueprint and nature's design. With influences from Greece, Rome, and the West Indies, you'll find comforts of home mixed with Old World Charm. Whether you are ambling through charming downtown areas; biking along many of the nature trails; or strolling in the colorful flora and fauna; you'll be charmed by the beauty of the area.

The best way to enjoy the flavor of these wonderful seaside retreats is to drive the 18-mile path on Scenic Hwy. 30A. Along this beautiful stretch, you will encounter stunning sights and lovely landmarks. This excursion will take you through several seaside communities, and you'll be able to experience the rich countryside. Take advantage of the great picnic opportunities along the way!

CARILLON BEACH

This is one of those sleepy little "paradise" beaches where time seems to stand still—at least long enough for you to fall in love with its beauty and serenity. It is advertised as, "a world apart," and does indeed seem to be isolated from the busyness of the real world. Its almost picture-perfect quality comes from very detailed planning and a lot of help from nature. Carillon Beach was created in

1982, and developed by the William Biggs Sr. family. This family had the vision to create a community that would be sensitive to the environment, as well as develop a place that would draw families year after year. It is 104-acres of gulf-front property located off of Hwy. 98 in Bay County, that includes a 12-acre lake; several naturally-landscaped parks; three swimming pools; tennis courts; and, of course, the famous powder white beaches of the Gulf of Mexico. Everything is within walking distance, so you will feel "close to home" and right in the middle of the lives of the townspeople.

The "neighborhood" was created with the influences of ancient Greece and Rome—a pedestrian community with an active downtown area. It is filled with shops, galleries, restaurants, and lots of Old World Charm. Take a stroll down Market Street in search of exciting treasures.

ROSEMARY BEACH

Rosemary Beach, which was named for the herb that is indigenous to the area, is a planned community that transports elements of the West Indies to the Florida Panhandle. Established in 1995, this stunning village effortlessly weaves family homes, courtyards, parks, and meandering footpaths into its landscape. Inspired by the small, waterfront towns of the Caribbean, the homes and buildings of Rosemary Beach bring the warmth of the Gulf breezes inside. You'll find high ceilings, sleeping porches, ceiling fans, and open balconies. Only steps from the pristine shores, this unique community nestles around a lively town center. Within a five-minute walk (or less) from anywhere in Rosemary Beach, you'll find the area's treasures—specialty shops, restaurants, European-style Bed and Breakfasts, and even a West Indies Market. The pace of life here is, as you might imagine, breezy, casual, and intimate—definitely fitting for the Gulf.

SEAGROVE BEACH

Seagrove Beach, with its charming beach cottages for vacationers, was once a navigational point for sailors because it could be seen a mile out at sea. You will adore its antique shops, art galleries, and quaint seaside appeal. The water is assorted shades of turquoise; the sand is as fine as powder; and the breezes are refreshing. You'll see pelicans swooping into the Gulf waters for an afternoon snack, as well as seagulls playing along the shore. But, that might be all you see, because Seagrove Beach is somewhat secluded. Your stay here will be a beautiful and cherished memory.

For more information on Carillon Beach, Rosemary Beach or Seagrove Beach, visit the Beaches of South Walton Tourist Development Council at www.beachesofsouthwalton.com or call 800-822-6877 or 850-267-1216.

Seagrove Beach Fairs Festivals & Fun

May
    Arts Quest

DOWNTOWN CARILLON BEACH

Nestled in the heart of the Emerald Coast at the west end of Panama City Beach, and just east of the Phillips Inlet Bridge, Downtown Carillon offers a great mix of shops, restaurants, concerts, and fun for the entire family. With its New Orleans-style shopping, you'll need an extra suitcase for all your purchases. Feeling hungry? Stop by The Café on Lake Carillon, Bamboo Billys Tiki Hut or the Hava Java Coffee Shop. Besides offering great food, Bamboo Billys serves up entertainment from the area's finest musicians, as well as canoe and paddleboat rides on beautiful Lake Carillon. You'll also want to check out the "Banana Cabanas" in the Calypso Courtyard for a unique mix of eclectic items and cool snacks for the entire family.

The Merchants of Market Street pride themselves on offering the finest quality goods in the area. The merchant line-up includes: Beachwalk Birkenstock; Sterling Shores Silver Jewelry and Gifts; Gidgets; Bungalows; Patina—contemporary arts and crafts; Shipwreck, Ltd; General Store; and Lacey Grace Gourmet Candy Shoppe.

Stop by the new Carillon Beach Rental office and Internet Café and rent a beautiful beach home; a Market Street townhouse; or a loft condominium.

To find out more about Downtown Carillon Beach, call 850-234-5600 or visit www.Carillon-Beach.com online.

collaborations

Collaborations, 4721 E. Scenic Hwy. 30A, Ste. E, is just that . . . a collaboration of the entire community of Seagrove Beach. Owners Bobby Johnson and Ty Sims literally let the community decide what they sell. You will find everything from exquisite antiques and primitives to consigned pieces of art. They purchase new merchandise constantly, and with the consignments, they never know what the store will look like from one week to the next. That just makes it more fun, and it keeps the customers coming often. Collaborations is open daily 10 am-6 pm. Stop by for a cup of great coffee while you shop. Call 850-231-0171 or visit www.collabart.com online.

The Gourd Garden
and curiosity shop

Just a stone's throw from the Gulf of Mexico and two miles east of Seaside, you'll find the most unforgettable place. Here gourd vines twine through rustic arbors and wrens nest in a collection of unique gourd birdhouses. The Gourd Garden & Curiosity Shop is the creation of Randy Harelson, a Louisiana artist who has combined his love of art and horticulture into one profession at 4808 E. Co. Hwy. 30A in Seagrove Beach. You'll find folk art from around the world; handmade pottery; gourds; books; cards; body luxuries; organic gardening products;

tools; toys; and native plants, herbs and flowers from the Deep South. You can also purchase seed for your own "gourd garden." The shop is open Monday-Saturday 9 am-5 pm and Sunday noon-5 pm. Call 850-231-2007 or visit www.gourdgarden.com.

PICKETS

When in Seagrove Beach, this is a must visit. Owner Jo Ann Mathis, with the help of her mom, created a beautiful cottage garden that welcomes you into Pickets. Husband Jim built picket fences, arbors and pergolas, which add to the charm of Pickets. As you stroll past the picket fence and down the winding path to the lovely 1952 cottage you will feel the warmth of a beach home. Pickets has been featured in *Mary Englebreit's Home Companion* and *Southern Living Vacations* magazines.

The store itself offers the latest in garden whimsy, and home décor. Always available are vintage tablecloths; lamps; rugs; baskets; as well as a great selection of birdhouses, bunnies and other garden accessories.

Pickets is located at 10 Nightcap St. on the corner of Nightcap and 30A, and is open Tuesday through Saturday from 10 am-5 pm. For more information, call 850-231-2036.

THE PENSIONE AT ROSEMARY BEACH

This handsome, sophisticated Bed & Breakfast at 78 Main St., draws its inspiration from the "pensiones" or inexpensive tourist havens in Italy. It was designed by University of Miami professors Luis and Jorge Trelles, who transformed Mark and Penny Dragonnette's ideas into a charming eight-room European Inn located just steps from the Gulf of Mexico. The Dragonettes had traveled throughout Italy, and loved staying at the many "pensiones," throughout the country. They wanted to bring a little of that romantic, historical atmosphere to the design of their bed and breakfast inn. Mission accomplished. The Pensione at Rosemary Beach offers guests a relaxed atmosphere, breath-taking views, and the luxury of a pricey resort at very reasonable rates. All rooms feature private baths and queen-sized beds, and all are appointed with original paintings and artwork by Dee Van Dyke. Included in your stay is a continental breakfast served in the restaurant on the first floor, which is also open for lunch and dinner. For reservations, call 850-231-1790 or visit www.thepensione.com.

"Where you are treated like family"

How would you like to go on vacation but still feel at home? The moment you walk through the doors of Beach Rentals of South Walton, you immediately get that feeling. With a welcoming lobby filled with friendly staff plus a children's play area, it's easy to see why their motto is, "Where you're treated like family." From their small and cozy condos to their luxurious private beach homes, you'll love the surrounding area—full of prime shopping, restaurants, bike rentals, and the most beautiful beaches in the world. Located at 5311 E. Co. Hwy. 30A in Seagrove Beach, this family-run business has definitely put the word "service" back into the industry. Open daily 8 am-5 pm during the summer. For more information, call 888-541-0801 or visit www.beachrentalsofsouthwalton.com.

Since its opening in 1995, Café Thirty-A has consistently been named by *Florida Trend Magazine* as a Golden Spoon award winner, and its extensive wine list has garnered an Award of Excellence from *Wine Spectator Magazine* every year since 1996. Owner Harriet Crommelin graciously says, "The whole staff is like family, and so are our customers." She credits this great personal customer attention for the reason Café Thirty-A is a Seagrove Beach favorite for casual, yet sophisticated, fine dining. That might be one reason, but wait until you taste the food! Café Thirty-A offers fresh fish, top-quality meats and poultry, and oven-fired pizzas. Outstanding entrees include pan-seared sesame crusted tuna with Asian stirfry; crispy duck with lentils and mission figs; and grilled filet mignon with porcini mushroom sauce and blue cheese foam. Hedonistic desserts such as crème brulee and banana beignets add the perfect ending to an unforgettable meal. And, don't forget to start with one of Café Thirty-A's famous martinis! The restaurant is located at 3899 E. Scenic Hwy. 30A, approximately 1.5 miles east of Seaside. Café Thirty-A is open daily for dinner at 6 pm. For more information, call 850-231-2166 or visit www.cafethirtya.com online.

When husband and wife, George and Ann Hartley, moved to Florida to enjoy "a simple life at the beach," they had no idea they would one day own one of the most popular haunts in Seagrove Beach.

As a deli, grocery and café, the Seagrove Village MarketCafé is a favorite meeting place for locals and a hot spot for year-round visitors.

Nestled in a homey setting, the 54-year-old building was the original "mom and pop" grocery and gas station run out of a house. Although the Seagrove Village MarketCafé, 3004 S. Hwy. 395, has come along way since then, it never lost its welcoming homey feel.

Whether you're enjoying a grouper or Po-Boy sandwich, always expect a hearty side of Southern hospitality and charm on the side. For more information, call 850-231-5736. *(Color picture featured in front section of the book.)*

Cowgirl Kitchen

If there were ever a place that could "take the cowgirl out of Texas" it would be the beautiful Emerald Coast. After vacationing in Destin, Nancy Dupre-Scarborough fell in love with the area, and moved her very successful catering and "food-to-go" business to 4281 E. Hwy. 30A in Seagrove Beach. She began her business in Dallas, after seeing a need for quick lunches. She started taking baskets and box lunches to offices at lunchtime, and soon opened her store. The Cowgirl Kitchen menu includes great sandwiches; fresh salads; soups (whatever she feels like making that day); and too many desserts to list. Try the Chicken Spaghetti, King Ranch Chicken, or Beef Stroganoff, for a quick dinner. And, use the specialty dips for easy entertaining. We loved the Cream Corn Jalapeno Dip! The kitchen is open Monday-Saturday 10 am-6 pm. For more information, call 850-231-7877.

FRESH SEAFOOD MARKET

Who is Captain Zac? Well, he's not a salty old sailor from the seven seas. Or is he? Actually, Zac is the son of Nickoel Ard, owner of Capt. Zac's Fresh Seafood Market, 4935 E. Co. Hwy. 30A. You may get lucky and see him around when you visit this market of fresh seafood, bait, and other groceries. Located between Seaside and Rosemary, Capt. Zac's is a great place to get fresh seafood. They'll even steam it for you—free of charge! Market hours are Monday-Thursday 10 am-7 pm and Friday-Sunday 9 am-7 pm. Call 850-231-5954.

DISCOVER
FORT WALTON BEACH /
NAVARRE BEACH / SHALIMAR

Do you have a thirst for history, a love for visiting the paths that were laid by people years ago? If so, then you'll adore the area surrounding Fort Walton Beach and Navarre. You'll stand in the same spots as prehistoric people, see the land that drew pirates for centuries, and visit areas that were vital during the Civil War.

Of course, mix this rich history with the sunny splendor of the Emerald Coast, and you'll be in heaven. From the white, Appalachian quartz sand that blankets the beaches to the barrier islands that protect Florida's coast, it's a divine vacation destination.

FORT WALTON BEACH

Yesterday and Today

One of the best ways to get a glimpse of the Fort Walton Beach area is to visit old downtown Fort Walton Beach. With its wonderful shops, antiques, cafes, and numerous museums, it's a perfect place to hang out. Restaurants and nightclubs add excitement to a long day's fishing trip, and kids will love visiting the Gulfarium and amusement parks scattered along the seashore.

Fort Walton Beach lies only seven miles from Destin and offers the incredible natural beauty of the Emerald Coast—with prices a little less expensive than its neighbors. Families are drawn to Fort Walton because there are so many exciting activities. There are marine animal parks, zoo parks, water parks, miniature golf, snorkeling, canoeing, and golfing. You might enjoy a bicycle ride through the State Park or along the lakes and charming settlements. You'll not only enjoy the area, but you'll also enjoy the people. The locals don't just live "the beach life," they also run the businesses you will visit. They are colorful, happy, and very welcoming to their guests.

Blending old and new, ancient and modern—that's what Fort Walton Beach does best. Though the Fort Walton Beach municipality was created in 1937, the history of the area is much older.

Rich In History

In the center of downtown Fort Walton Beach, you'll find an Indian Temple Mound, which dates back to 12,000 B.C. This mound, along with other village remains, is from several cultures. In fact, Fort Walton Beach boasts of having "the most significant archaeological resources in the Panhandle area."

The area was also a favorite haunt of pirates during the 16th-19th centuries. With many coves and bays, it provided the perfect place for hiding. The most famous pirate to sail these waters was Billy Bowlegs. In fact, Fort Walton Beach celebrates his legend with an annual festival each summer.

During the Civil War, Fort Walton Beach housed an encampment for the Confederate Walton Guards, which protected it from sea invasion by Union forces. Today, the Fort Walton Beach area still houses military bases: Hurlburt Field and Eglin Air Force Base.

Following the Civil War, John Thomas Brooks, Fort Walton Beach's founder, returned to the area and built the first hotel, Brooks House. Because of his humanitarian contributions, the city was first named Brooks' Landing. Its name later changed to Camp Walton after Colonel George Walton. Then in 1941, its name changed to the City of Fort Walton, and again in 1953, it changed to Fort Walton Beach.

With its rich history and relaxing beauty, you and your family are sure to find the perfect pastime to make your Fort Walton Beach vacation unforgettable.

NAVARRE BEACH

For Namesake

This beach community hugs the emerald-green waters of the Gulf of Mexico with sand so beautiful that locals tell us visitors refer to it as sugar. Navarre is particularly known for its spectacular sand dunes. The warm Gulf breezes constantly stir and shift the sand so that the dunes appear to be "rolling."

Established in 1925, Navarre was settled by Colonel Guy H. Wyman. It was, in fact, his wife who named this quaint town after her favorite Spanish province. Navarre remained relatively unknown until the early 1960s when the Navarre Beach Bridge was constructed. This bridge opened the pristine beaches of the Gulf Coast on Santa Rosa Island. Since then, Navarre has attracted numerous visitors.

The Great Outdoors

Great activities abound to keep everyone happy. For those who want to laze on the beach and do nothing at all to those who are more energetic—Navarre Beach has it all! A 2003 addition was the Navarre Beach State Park, offering camping; swimming; and a planned marine sanctuary. There are lots of rental shops for jet skis, wind surfers, paddleboats, and parasail rides. And, the newly-renovated Navarre Fishing Pier holds hours of great fun for anglers of all ages. They will love being able to reel in pompano, grouper, cobia, king and Spanish mackerel right from the pier!

We know that you will agree that Navarre Beach is a dream come true for vacationers.

SHALIMAR

Where It All Began

The name "Shalimar" is said to mean "by the beautiful water." Of course this is an understatement anywhere here on the remarkable Emerald Coast. A 1944 article in the Atlanta Journal read …"The little town of Shalimar is a world of its own."

It was actually begun during the early 1940s as military housing. Mr. Clifford Meigs built 160 little cottages in an area many considered to be "too remote" or "way out in the woods." As soon as the war was over and the military moved out, tourists began to find their way to this private part of Florida, "by the beautiful water," and the community of Shalimar began to grow. Although the population has doubled since the 1980s, it really hasn't grown too much since the 1940s. That in itself is one thing that makes it so enticing to visitors. It is still a "small town community" with only around 700 local residents. In fact, a permanent structure on Eglin Parkway near the Town Hall announces town activities and residents' birthdays!

For more information on Fort Walton Beach, call the Emerald Coast Convention and Visitors Bureau at 800-322-3319 or 850-651-1131 or visit www.destin-fwb.com online.

For more information on Navarre Beach, visit www.beaches-rivers.com online or call the Navarre Beach Chamber of Commerce at 800-480-SAND or 850-939-3267.

For more information on Shalimar, visit www.shalimarflorida.org online.

Fort Walton Beach / Navarre
Fairs Festivals & Fun

January
Antique Show & Sale
Emerald Coast Concert Association, Jan-Mar
NWFL Philharmonic, Jan-Mar Season
Navarre Beach Run
Senior Snowbird Expo

February
Beaux Arts Exhibition
AKC Dog Show, NWFL Fairgrounds
Taste of the Bayou
Mardi Gras On the Island
Taste of Fort Walton Beach
Navarre's Mardi Gras Parade

March
Florida Sportsman Fishing Show
Home Show, OWCC
Old Spanish Trail Festival
Archaeology Day, Indian Museum
Gulfarium's Birthday Bash
ABWA Car Show

April
Navarre's Abitaman Triathlon
Musical Echoes
Saturday in the Park, Heritage Museum
Community Earth Day
Cobia Tournament
St. Mary's Spring Fling
Founder's Day Celebration

May

Blessing of the Fleet
May Day
Okaloosa County Student Art Show
Community Chorus Spring Program
Coast Guard Open House
Classic & Wooden Boat Show
Scottish Festival
Tourism Week
Billy Bowlegs Poker Run
Sunday in the Park, FWB
Navarre Parade of Homes

June

Soundside Bridal Show
Summer Concert Series
Wyland Poker Run
Sprint Billy Bowlegs Festival
Navarre's "Fun Fest"
Kid's Day
Surf & Turf Championships
Parade of Homes

July

American Tribute Concert
July 4th Festivities & Bike Parade
Kid's Day
Independence Day Festivities

August

Emerald Coast Boat Week
Greek Festival
Brewfest
King Mackerel Tournament

September

NWFL Doll Show
Crestview Music Festival
Emerald Coast Car Show
Round the Island Race
MidBay Bridge Run/Walk
Sunday in the Park

October
    BWB Oktoberfest
    Holly Fair
    First Arts Concert Series, Oct-Mar Season
    Rally of Eagles, Model Airplanes
    Hobie Continental Championships
    Boggy Bayou Mullet Festival
    Festa Italiana
    NWFL Fair & Fine Art Show
    Fishing Rodeo
    Navarre Beach Realtors Car Show
    Zoo Boo
    Beaches to Woodlands Tour

November
    Kevin Green Charity Golf Tournament
    Armed Forces Appreciation Day
    Emerald Coast Martial Arts Championships
    Winter Wondersand
    Taste of the Emerald Coast
    Holiday Lights at the Zoo
    Camellia Show
    St. Simon's Craft Bazaar

December
    Camp Walton Schoolhouse Holiday Open House
    Christmas in the Park
    Florida State Chili Championship

Antiques

DARBY-MITCHELL ANTIQUES

A personal touch is what you will experience at Darby-Mitchell Antiques. With more than 30 years in the antique business, Gerald Darby knows how to find the "best of the best." Gerald, with the help of his sister, makes frequent trips to Europe to personally select every piece. He and his sister have made these trips for the past 20 years. While 18th and 19th century furniture and accessories are their specialty, that's not all you'll see on display here at 158 Miracle Strip Pkwy. in what is known as the Historical District of Fort Walton Beach, just across from the Indian Mound Museum. Darby-Mitchell Antiques also offers its clients an all-encompassing design-service. From locating one special piece to furnishing a total quality interior—Darby-Mitchell has you covered! It is because of this full service treatment that Darby-Mitchell Antiques has become one of the largest and finest antique businesses in the South. Call 850-244-4069 or visit www.darby-mitchellantiques.com online. Hours are Monday-Saturday 10 am-5 pm and by appointment on Sunday.

SWEET JODY'S ANTIQUE MALL

Long time locals might recognize the name *Sweet Jody* as a favorite deep-sea fishing boat, because the Godwins are Florida natives with many generations of boat captains and charter boats. With this rich family history, it only seemed right when Jody Godwin opened her antique store to name it after a boat. Located at 205 Florida Pl. S.E.—1 block north of Hwy. 98 on Eglin Pkwy.—in the downtown, historic section of Fort Walton Beach, Sweet Jody's is one of the most fun and exciting places to shop for wonderful antiques and uniques. In keeping with the "old is better" theme, Sweet Jody's is located in a 1940s era building restored by the Godwin family to win a "Beautification Award" from the city of Fort Walton Beach in 2003.

You'll find something for every age and imagination tucked into the corners of Sweet Jody's—new and used collectibles; vintage clothing and jewelry; wonderful antiques; old books; priceless toys; art deco furniture; and retro home decorations; from the 40s, 50s, 60s and 70s. In keeping with the fishing heritage, Jody always seems to have a lot of nautical pieces.

Special sections of the store are: an art gallery and artist's studio with beautiful water color and acrylic artwork by locally famous painters; used book store, one of only two in the area; and a coffee shop in the midst of all the treasures. With more than 30 vendors, you will enjoy an ever-changing selection of wonderful gifts. Sweet Jody's motto is: "Why buy any ol' gift, when you can buy a gift with a story?"

Look for the bright red awning, the white picket fence and the smartly dressed mannequins near the road! Open Monday-Saturday, 9 am to 5 pm with extended hours in the summer months. Visit www.sweetjody.com or call 850-664-6445.

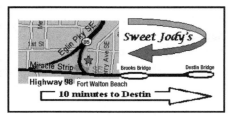

Attractions & Entertainment

GULFARIUM

In 1954, the unspoiled pristine beaches of South Okaloosa County were largely undiscovered. It was then that Brandy Siebenaler, a graduate student from the University of Miami, visited the Northwest Florida area to further his Marine Science studies. It was during this visit that Brandy discovered the 10-acre site that has been home to Florida's Gulfarium since 1954. The continuous operation since then acknowledges Florida's Gulfarium as "The oldest marine show aquarium in the world."

Don Abrams, Gulfarium's General Manager, echoes Brandy's sentiments when he states; "Education as well as dolphin interaction and teaching our population how to respect our oceans and marine life was always Brandy's passion and dream." AND, HIS DREAM LIVES ON TODAY…

Visitors are entertained daily, rain or shine by the Dolphin Show, Sea Lion Show, Living Sea Theater and the Multi-Species Show. The Living Sea Theater features a scuba diver in a 50,000-gallon "salt water aquarium" with huge viewing panels and theater-style seating.

Exotic birds, American alligators, sharks, rays and more are featured in numerous pools and public exhibit areas on the grounds.

Other projects include; an Education Department, Summer Camp Programs, Spotted Dolphin Encounters, Birthday Parties, Corporate Outings and more. In 1999, the JF Dolphin Project was launched at Florida's Gulfarium. This program has been recognized as one of the finest "Special Needs" Therapy Programs for children. The JF Dolphin Project incorporates Dolphin-Assisted Therapy for autistic and Downs Syndrome children.

Can you imagine a California Sea Lion and 600-pound Pacific Bottlenose Dolphin kissing? How about this same Sea Lion giving up a fish to his Dolphin pal? Seeing is believing at the Multi-Species Show. As one of four continuous daily programs, the Multi-Species show is hailed as one of the best in the world!

Florida's Gulfarium is located at 1010 Miracle Strip Pkwy. S.E., in Fort Walton Beach. For information, call 800-247-8575 or 850-243-9046 or visit or www.gulfarium.com.

Dueling pianos? Absolutely! That's just one of the many things going on at Howl at the Moon. Located on the Boardwalk on Okaloosa Island (part of Fort Walton Beach) between the Ramada Plaza Beach Resort and Crab Shack, Howl at the Moon is the place to be for fun. It's a dueling piano, rock and roll show full of singing, hand clapping, foot stomping, and edge-of-your-seat entertainment. Whether you need a place to hold that special event or you simply want to go out for a night on the town, Howl at the Moon is fun for all ages 18 and up.

Hours are 7 pm-4 am Tuesday-Sunday. Every Sunday night at Howl at the Moon you'll find the area's only Comedy Zone. Come ready to laugh! The comedy show begins at around 9 pm after an hour or so of dueling pianos. Reservations are not required but available. Visit www.howlatthemoon.com online or call the information line at 850-301-0111.

AUNT MARTHA'S BED & BREAKFAST

Step into the foyer of this stately mansion and experience the gracious Southern charm of old Florida. Owners Martha and Bill Garvie hope you'll enjoy an unforgettable experience in their spectacular inn—Aunt Martha's Bed & Breakfast at 315 Shell Ave. S. E. in Fort Walton Beach. The rooms feature windows that open to the sounds of the shore and warm gulf breezes. And, a delicious breakfast is served each morning. Call 850-243-6702 or visit www.auntmarthasbedandbreakfast.com.

DALE E PETERSON VACATIONS

Navarre Beach, one of Florida's best-kept secrets, seems to her visitors an unspoiled paradise. It is surrounded by Santa Rosa Sound on the north, the Gulf of Mexico on the south, and by federal land preserves to the east and west. It comes pretty close to being just about the perfect place to vacation. In contrast, it is no secret at all that one of the best-known vacation rental and real estate companies on the Emerald Coast is Dale E. Peterson Vacations. It has grown through the years into one of the top agencies in the business, and promotes the Navarre Beach area with enthusiasm. Its friendly and professional staff offers properties from Navarre Beach to Panama City Beach—everything from studio and penthouse condominiums to cozy cottages and sprawling beach houses.

Navarre Beach has been ranked one of the best in America for its sand quality, sunny days, gentle currents, and uncrowded atmosphere. There is a one-mile scenic trail along the sound and great pier fishing. If this sounds perfect for your next vacation, let Dale E. Peterson Vacations make your fantasy a reality. For more information, stop by the office at 8721 Gulf Blvd., call 800-336-9669 or 850-654-4747, or visit www.destinresorts.com.

LINDA RANDES/
ERA AMERICAN REALTY OF NW FLORIDA, INC.

When you choose Linda Randes as your Realtor, you are not only receiving the expertise of someone who has lived in the area all of her life but also partnering with the No. 1 agent at American Realty and with a national company offering the client the ultimate in real estate service. Linda's office is located at 1270 N. Eglin Pkwy. in Shalimar in an office building with a "history!" It used to be "The Shalimar Club," a nightclub and gambling casino. Take advantage of Randes' incredible contacts throughout the area and the support of a wonderfully successful team for all of your real estate needs. Call Linda direct at 850-585-4085.

Alyce's
FLORAL DESIGNS

Meeting owners Elaine and Albert Ridge will give you an idea as to why Alyce's Floral Designs in Fort Walton Beach is so well loved. Their motto is "Never underestimate the power of a flower." Elaine and staff of experienced designers will help you create the perfect arrangement or gift basket for any occasion. The Ridges are very community-minded, and have been given several awards for their willingness to share their creative gifts with those in need. Visit Alyce's at 224F Eglin Pkwy. from 8 am-5 pm Monday-Friday and until 1 pm on Saturday. For more information, call 850-862-8331 or 850-862-8332. Visit www.alycesfloraldesign.com or e-mail powerofaflower.com.

BARBARA SLOCUMB DESIGNS

Barbara Slocumb has more than 23 years experience as a detailed wedding consultant/planner and florist. You can trust her with personal service in specializing wedding plans and festive celebrations. As a local, long-time resident, Barbara has all the "insider info" for planning your event! Her elegant and unique floral service includes garden style, shabby chic, tabletop topiaries, along with fruit and flower garlands. References are available upon request. Call 850-651-3311 or fax 850-651-7894.

BASKETHOUND GIFT SHOP

Betty Jernigan and Trudy Goddin are business partners, mom and daughter, and each other's biggest supporters. Their darling gift shop at 1821 Alpine Ave. in Navarre is filled with items such as balloons, flowers, gourmet foods, coffees, and unique specialty gifts. Whatever the occasion, they have the perfect goodies to fill a customized gift basket decorated just for you. You'll also find Betty's handiwork—beautiful silk flower arrangements, wreaths, pillows, and hand-painted furniture. They deliver locally and can ship too! Open Monday-Friday 9 am-5:30 pm and Saturday 10 am-2 pm. Later hours during holidays. Call 850-936-1119.

Couch and Four Gifts

It is a "treasure chest" in the heart of the Emerald Coast; a favorite of locals and tourists since 1968; and a shop you mustn't miss on your Lady's Day Out in Fort Walton Beach. Located in the historic waterfront district at 130 Miracle Strip Pkwy., Coach and Four Gifts is an absolute delight! This 8,000-square-foot store offers one of the largest selections of gifts; collectibles; decorative accessories; and gourmet kitchen products in Northwest Florida. (Hope you brought an empty suitcase!)

Owners Doug and Michelle Murphy enjoy the company of so many faithful, loyal, local customers, and an ever-surprising and increasing number of repeat vacationers. They often hear, "We never miss a visit to your store when we visit the area," or "Coach and Four is our favorite store!" That's music to the Murphys' ears. Our favorite part of the store? The divine homemade fudge—made with real cream and butter—right in the store. Coach and Four Gifts is open 9:30 am-6 pm, Monday-Saturday and Sunday noon-5 pm. Call 850-243-1721 for more informtion.

PAPILLON'S OF NAVARRE

This bright and beautiful gift shop, 1888 Andorra St. in the Publix Shopping Center, is named for the delicate butterfly, and it's as fun and fancy as its name. Owner Susan Finnan has filled it with all of the things she loves, including: sterling silver jewelry, specialty lamps, diaries and backpack purses for pre-teens. She carries seasonal gifts for Mardi Gras, Valentine's Day, Easter, fall holidays and, of course, Christmas. You'll also find causal dishes, serving pieces, candlesticks, placemats and napkins. We loved the picnic baskets complete with fishnet wine bottle bags. Papillon's of Navarre is open Monday-Friday 10 am-5 pm, and Saturday until 3 pm. Call 850-936-8659.

Mary K. Haik learned to garden at a very early age, and has known since then that she would be happiest with her hands "in the dirt!" For years, she imagined creating a comfortable place for people to find interesting, useful items for the home and garden in a relaxing, artsy setting. Her three daughters are her partners in one of the most adorable, whimsical, and fun home and garden shops in Florida. Marigold's, 228 Troy St. in Fort Walton Beach, is an eclectic combination of "greening gifts;" creative and custom jewelry; unique crosses; fantastic pottery; and both local and national fine art. Their flower arrangements are exciting and unique, and even the gift-wrap brings smiles of joy to the receiver. Mary K. also shares her enthusiasm for creative gardening by offering classes and workshops. You'll enjoy the wonderful items tucked in every corner. Hours are Monday-Saturday 9:30 am-5:30 pm. Call 850-244-4920.

If you are looking for the perfect gift, hard-to-find collectible, or something unique and special for your home, Designs and Accessories at 1104 N. Eglin Pkwy. in Shalimar, should be your first stop. This beautiful new building has more than 5,000-square-feet of shopping area; so just imagine all of the wonderful things you'll find inside! The entire second floor is reserved for stock, so the shelves are always full of new and exciting items. One of the newest additions is the collection of beautiful fragrance lamps by La Maison Du Parfumeur. Other popular lines include Camille Beckman Bath & Body Products; Hummel figurines; Boyds Bears; and over 75 feet of jewelry. Plan to spend some time here, because there is much to see. Designs and Accessories is open Monday-Saturday 9 am-5 pm. Visit www.designsandaccessories.com or call 850-651-3324.

VANDEGRIFF JEWELERS

Vandegriff Jewelers, at 131 Racetrack Rd. N.W. in Fort Walton Beach, is one of the premier jewelry stores on the Emerald Coast, and the history behind it is as precious as the brilliant diamonds they sell. Harry and Margaret Vandegriff began their jewelry business in 1947, in a post war economy, with a newborn daughter. Margaret said that sometimes the only sale of the day was a 50¢ jar of silver polish!

The secret to their incredible success through the years has been their dedication to treating every customer with the utmost respect, and their daughter, Pat Balanzategui, carries on that tradition today as owner. They showcase the beautiful Hearts on Fire diamonds, as well as the unique Kosta Boda Fine Art Glass from Sweden. Trust Vandegriff's with your every jewelry need. Open Monday-Friday 9:30 am-5:30 pm, 9:30 am-4 pm on Saturday. Call 850-243-3333.

For a look at one of the most unique stores in Uptown Station, make sure to drop in at Garden of Beadin' in Fort Walton Beach at 99 Eglin Pkwy. #19 or in Destin 34904 Emerald Coast Pkwy. With countless types and colors of beads and crystals from all over the world, each customer is bound to leave with a little something special.

Whether you make it yourself or choose a beautifully-designed piece on display, chances are no one will have a piece of jewelry exactly like yours. Of course, jewelry isn't the only thing that comes beaded here! Browse around and choose from a selection of beaded flip-flops, wire-wrapped glasses, unique gift ideas as well as personalized items while you wait.

Open Monday-Friday 10 am-6 pm and Saturday 10 am-5 pm. Call 850-796-3262 in Fort Walton Beach or 850-654-4966 in Destin or visit www.gardenofbeadin.net for more information.

No man or woman
is worth your tears,
and the one who is,
won't make you cry.
—*Unknown*

Restaurants

MAGNOLIA GRILL OF FORT WALTON BEACH

 Tom and Peggy Rice have incorporated the history of early Fort Walton Beach along with their own significant family history in the beautiful Magnolia Grill at 157 Brooks St. S.E. The restaurant is located in one of the oldest buildings in the area, which was built as a mail order house. Visitors enjoy the historical memorabilia throughout the house, including many items of interest from Dr. and Mrs. J. H. Beal who were influential in changing the name of the town from Camp Walton to Fort Walton Beach. Even the menu is somewhat "historical." Several items on the menu originated in local restaurants from the past. The food is wonderful, and the atmosphere is unforgettable. The Magnolia Grill is open Monday-Thursday 11 am-2 pm and 5-8 pm; Friday until 9 pm; and Saturday 5-9 pm for dinner only. Call 850-302-0266 or visit www.magnoliagrillfwb.com online.

 **Seafood Restaurant**

 Located at 24 Miracle Strip Pkwy. S.E. in Fort Walton Beach, this historic restaurant is one of Florida's oldest, continuously family-owned restaurants. The Staff family immigrated to America from Czechoslovakia during the 1800s when the family name "Stech" or "Steck" translated to "Staff." Theo Staff settled his family along the beautiful waters of the Gulf Coast in what was then called Fort Walton, and started in the hotel business. As guests began to return again and again for the fresh, deliciously prepared seafood dishes, he opened Staff's Restaurant—the first restaurant in Fort Walton Beach. The family takes great pride in the freshness of the seafood and produce. Seafood is purchased right off the boat from the local fishermen, and is cleaned and prepared by Staff's cooks. All fruits and vegetables are selected from the local produce markets each morning, and the delicious whole wheat breads are baked daily from a recipe dating back 70 years.

Staff's menu includes delicious appetizers such as Crabmeat Stuffed Mushrooms or Shrimp Quesadillas, and hearty soups like Seafood Gumbo or Seafood Bisque. Seafood dishes include almost any fish or shellfish you can name—from lobster, shrimp, or scallops to snapper, amberjack, or flounder. Stuffed, baked, fried, or grilled—order it the way you love it! Staff's Restaurant is open for dinner at 5 pm, and on the weekend nights, you'll enjoy live music in the lounge. One of the things you will love most about your meal is the extraordinary dessert bar in a unique boat display, and even better—it's free with your meal. Call 850-243-3482 or visit www.staffsrestaurant.com online.

PANDORA'S STEAK HOUSE AND LOUNGE

Whether you love steaks, prime rib, or seafood, you will absolutely enjoy every last bite when you dine at Pandora's Steak House, 1120 Santa Rosa Blvd. in Fort Walton Beach. The atmosphere is warm and welcoming, nothing fussy or overdone.

The appetizers are wonderful, and large enough to almost be a meal, but save room because it only gets better from here. Some of Pandora's most popular appetizers include the Bacon Wrapped Scallops and the Fried Eggplant topped with a creamy sauce of Andouille Sausage Crawfish. For dinner, choose from specials featuring lamb, veal, seafood, and, of course, excellent steaks and prime rib. Pandora's uses only the best quality beef, which is grilled over oak. From the favorite filet mignon to the grilled New York Strip, all steaks are grilled to order. All courses come with a baked potato and salad, but you'll also love the crisp sweet onion rings.

With a great meal, you will appreciate that Pandora's will be able to produce the perfect wine, from a Sauvignon Blanc with the appetizers, to a hearty Cabernet Sauvignon for the T-Bone. In fact, *Wine Spectator* has given Pandora's the Award of Excellence six years in a row. Let the staff help you with your wine selection.

Hopefully, you've saved room for the best—moist bread pudding served with Myer's dark rum sauce. Add coffee and a sip of Chambord, and you have finished the perfect meal. Dining at Pandora's is a leisurely treat, and one that you'll want to savor. You won't be at all surprised to learn that the restaurant is a four-star establishment. Open daily 5 am to 10 pm but closed Mondays Labor Day through Memorial Day. Call 850-244-8669.

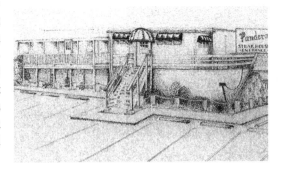

THE CRAB TRAP

Be sure and check out The Crab Trap in Fort Walton Beach, 1450 Miracle Strip Pkwy. See page 45 for full details or call 850-302-0959.

MULHOLLOWS BISTRO 2•1•5

Be sure and check out Mulhollows Bistro 215 in Fort Walton Beach at 215 Miracle Strip Parkway. See page 44 for full details.

MORE–NOT FISHY COOKING TIPS

Shrimp—buy with heads on. The heads are so easy to snap off later and your shrimp will be moister! Boil shrimp about 3 1/2 minutes, just until the shell separates from the body of the shrimp. Remember, you can always boil more! An owner of a fabulous old restaurant in New Orleans advises putting nothing in the water when boiling seafood for dishes. Add a few drops of sesame oil if you want to help with the aroma. Be careful: the 1/2 lb per person rule still applies, but remember the weight of the heads if buying heads-on.

—Peggy Adams

Come and experience serenity in this quaint tranquil environment located in downtown Fort Walton Beach. Serenity By The Sound Salon & Spa, 184 S.E. Brooks St., is a beautiful, and intimate salon, and Maria's personal attention will make it your favorite. When Maria Blaeser's mom came home one day to find Maria cutting and bleaching the hair of her Barbie dolls, she knew her daughter would someday have her own salon. Customers call a day with Maria "heavenly," so she named her package deals appropriately. Half Day of Heaven includes: manicure, pedicure, facial, hairstyle, and lunch with wine and flowers. For more heaven, opt for a Whole Day of Heaven or Make Over Day in Heaven. Also, ask about the permanent make-up and massage therapy. Hours are Tuesday-Wednesday 9 am-5 pm; Thursday-Friday 9 am-6 pm; and Saturday until 3 pm. For more information or for a late appointment, call 850-243-6119.

ABOUT FACE THERAPEUTIC SKIN CARE CENTER

Billie Smith started About Face more than 28 years ago when she couldn't find a place to get a facial, and her success has been astounding! Billie and her expertly trained staff love the fact that they can help transform lives by helping customers feel beautiful, refreshed, and invigorated. Come in and relax in comfortable, peaceful, private rooms while receiving one of many professional treatments. Treatments include: Glycolic Restoration; Microdermabrasion; Electrolysis; waxing; Laser hair removal; and Permanent Cosmetics. The salon is located at 907 N.W. Mar Walt Dr. in Fort Walton Beach. Hours vary call 850-862-2728 for appointments.

People have been seeking healing touch from Nicholas Night since he was nine years old. He lives out his dream everyday as his bodywork practice allows him to help others with anything from aches and pains to chronic and debilitating diseases. While Warm Hands offers an outstanding massage experience, many of Nick's clients find that their greatest relief and deepest relaxation comes from Craniosacral Therapy. This gentle, non-intrusive approach allows the client to remain clothed while long-standing tension patterns are released. Although impressed with the improvements in vitality, health, and mental and physical functioning they experience, most clients remark that the most astonishing, memorable thing about their sessions is the amount of caring they feel flowing into them from Nick's hands. Warm Hands (MA37184, MM12561) is located at 204 Martisa Rd. N.W. in Fort Walton Beach. Reservations are available Monday-Sunday 9 am-9 pm by calling 850-243-1573 or visiting www.warmhandsonline.com.

DISCOVER
GRAYTON BEACH / SEASIDE

GRAYTON BEACH

Inspirational Beauty

Grayton Beach began as a homestead in 1885, established by Army Major Charles T. Gray, and has pretty much remained a quiet, casual, private beach. It is a lovely picture of restored historic cottages, made of weathered cypress and bordered by beautiful trees. While visiting, you'll see that not much changes in Grayton Beach, and that includes its shoreline. Locals have fought fiercely to keep the high-rise developers from changing their intimate community. Its natural barriers and beautiful surrounding parklands have succeeded in protecting Grayton Beach from very much upscale development.

Many of the people you will meet here are long-time residents who have grown up on these beaches. They've watched each other's families grow, move away, and come home again. And, many of them would probably love for their beloved beach to remain their "private sanctuary."

Time does march on though, and with it brings change and inevitable growth. Grayton Beach has gently changed with the times, enticing more and more visitors each to year to discover her natural beauty and wonderful entertainment. New restaurants, gift shops, and planned recreational activities make Grayton Beach a perfect vacation place for the entire family.

SEASIDE

Dreams Can Come True

The story of Seaside's sweet beginnings is almost as beautiful as the golden place itself. It began a long time ago, during the childhood of Robert Davis. When he was a boy, Robert played on the beach, built cool sandcastles, and romped in the crystal waters every summer. He also loved cuddling up on the front porch of the beach house, listening to family stories, or playing board games. His favorite sandcastle-building partner was his beloved grandfather, J.S. Smolian, who purchased the 80 acres of beachfront property in 1946, when Robert was only 3 years old. The memories of these special summer times stayed with Robert and in the mid-1980s, he inherited the land from his grandfather.

As he and his wife Daryl began to travel and explore small towns, the idea of Seaside was born. They dreamed of a "beach town" that was simple and friendly; where the same families could summer together each year; a place to connect with nature and each other. Seaside became a reality with the land Mr. Smolian had purchased and bequeathed to Robert. It has grown beyond anything Robert and Daryl Davis could have imagined. It is a beautiful coastal town that mixes privacy and community, and it's filled with charming businesses that support the breezy, casual lifestyle of the place. Brick streets and picket fences border sweet rainbow-colored cottages. And, of course, they all have names (chosen by the owners) and front porches with rocking chairs! If this sounds vaguely familiar, you might remember the town as the site of "The Truman Show." Just as Robert remembers his heritage, families gather on the porches to talk, eat, and make their own memories that will carry them through the winters.

Shopping Extravaganza

In the middle of the community, you'll find a large amphitheater, which serves as the meeting place for picnics or evening entertainment. Surrounding the amphitheater are dozens (and we mean dozens!) of shops and cafes, boutiques, and an open-air market. You can walk to the market for your groceries; enjoy coffee and a pastry at a small café; or maybe stop in for a wine tasting and discussion. Visitors love the easy way of life here and the year-round events—they come back year after year to enjoy this little Camelot called Seaside.

For more information on Grayton Beach, visit www.graytonbeach.com online.

For more information on Seaside, visit www.seasidefl.com or call 888-SEASIDE.

For more information on both communities and the surrounding area, visit Beaches of South Walton at www.beachesofsouthwalton.com or call 800-822-6877 or 850-267-1216.

Seaside Fairs Festivals & Fun

February
   Community Yard Sale

March
   Cajun Concert

April
   Classic Car Show & Sock Hop
   Easter Parade & Activities

May
   Spring Wine Festival
   Memorial Day Weekend Activities
   Sunset Serenade Concert Series
   Summer Film Series, Friday Nights

June
   Storyteller
   Sunset Serenade Concerts
   Summer Film Series, Friday Nights

July
Storyteller
Sunset Serenade Concerts
Summer Film Series, Friday Nights
July 4th Parade & Weekend Activities

August
Storyteller
Sunset Serenade Concerts
Summer Film Series, Friday Nights
Labor Day Weekend Activities

September
Classic Film Series, Fridays
Endless Summer Saturday Concerts
Seaside's Annual Team Triathlon Adventure Race

October
Classic Film Series, Fridays
Via Colori
Community Yard Sale
Classic Car Show & Sock Hop
Safe Trick or Treat

November
Seeing Red Wine Festival
Holiday Parade and Turn on the Town

December
Strolling Carolers & Strolling Santas

ALBERT F
interiors

Brad and Holly Speight were tangled up in corporate America until 1999 when they decided to take Brad's father's advice to "follow your dream!" They had always loved the beautiful town of Seaside, and dreamed of one day opening a business there. Albert F Interiors in Seaside is the fruition of that dream, named after Brad's late father who inspired their new beginning in life. A Zen looking stone path curves at the flower garden to the entrance doors where you will be greeted by Holly and Brad's "canine kids" Max and Jack! Slate tile floors and walls and natural mahogany cabinets create a rich and elegant setting for their unique selection of gifts and home accessories. Brad's interior design business focuses on creating beautiful, yet comfortable living spaces. He has been featured in *Coastal Living Magazine* and *Southern Living Magazine*, and is well-known throughout the Southeast for his innovative design work. Albert F Interiors is located at 209 Ruskin Place in a building designed by the well-known New York City architect Walter Chatham. The shop is open Wednesday-Saturday 10 am-6 pm and Sunday noon-6 pm. Call 850-231-3497 or visit www.seasidefl.com.

iLHELMiNA

things old, new and blue

Even though Linda Eyer has traveled and lived throughout the world in exotic places like Tunisia, Belgium, Saudi Arabia, Bahrain, and Kuwait, her "heart home" has always been the beautiful bit of paradise called Grayton Beach. It is where she brought her children every summer for 30 years while living abroad so that they would have a sense of "home and roots," and it was the place she described to foreign friends who thought they had "seen" the United States because they had visited a major city. As a third generation family in Grayton Beach, Linda can remember cows and pigs roaming the sandy shores, but loves the unique and beautiful place it is today.

In Wilhelmina, Linda's lovely shop, at 26 Logan Ln., she shares the stories of the past and present in her eclectic collection. It is a charming combination of nostalgia and Southern hospitality. She carries local art and hand-made items, which give the store a one-of-a-kind personality. We loved the dragonflies and wooden crosses crafted from old wood and tin, and her exquisite collection of seashells from around the world—God's handi-work. The antiques and wonderful pieces of art throughout the shop give an instant comfort, warmth, and sense of "being home."

Linda chose her mother's name, "Wilhelmina," for her store and a picture of her mother as the logo. Her mother's managerial abilities and honest straightforwardness were her inspiration. Linda describes her "niche" as somewhere between yesterday and today—a resting place or a footpath between the two worlds of things old, new and blue! Hours are Monday-Saturday 10 am-5 pm. For more information, call 850-231-0737.

LYNN FIELD REDDOCH
INTERIOR DESIGN

Lynn Field Reddoch has emerged as one of the premiere interior designers on the Emerald Coast, and her work has been featured in more than 10 major publications. You will hear words like "innovative," "resourceful," "artistic," "ingenious," and "imaginative" used to describe this dynamic woman and her work. To give you an idea of her creativity, she used lime-based paint, and four 200-year-old doors from Monaco in her building at 119 Quincy Cir. in Seaside, making a relatively new building look very old. She makes headboards and chandeliers from Romanian iron pieces, and has filled her beautiful showroom with unique items from across the world. It is definitely not the average design or antique shop, because you will find very few items that can be bought at market.

While studying interior design at Parsons, Lynn found herself in the Art Student League, and had the privilege of studying portrait painting from Robert Brackman, known for his famous painting of Charles Lindberg. After working with Brackman she had the opportunity to work with Al Fine, restoring the Breakers—the Newport home of the Vanderbilts. Her talents are unlimited, and she has the capability to work in so many different mediums. One of the things customers love most about Lynn is her ability to incorporate their personalities and style into their interiors—whether contemporary or traditional, adding a surprising twist!

With more and more families making the Florida beaches their permanent homes, Lynn loves the challenge of making new condominiums appear lived in and comfortable, yet sophisticated and unique. For information, call 850-231-9117 or visit one of the sites online, www.lynnfieldreddoch.com, www.quincy@web30A.com.

PIZITZ HOME & COTTAGE

When Pizitz Home & Cottage started out in 1988, it was pretty much the "Seaside General Store." Customers could find everything from plumbing fixtures to Egyptian cotton sheets. Today, it's a gorgeous home furnishings store specializing in "Seaside style." You'll love the handcrafted farm tables, luxurious bed linens, and sensational slipcovered sofas and chairs. The on-site design workshop offers help with small refurbishings to large home design projects. Pizitz Home & Cottage will provide the luxuries and necessities for simple, comfortable Seaside living. Named for Seaside developer Robert Davis' grandfather Louis Pizitz, founder of the Pizitz Department Stores in Alabama, this store is fabulous! It is located in the Steven Holl Building at 121 Central Square in Seaside, and is open daily 10 am-6 pm and Memorial Day through Labor Day 10 am-9 pm. Call 850-231-2240.

Only Irish coffee
provides in a single cup
all four essential food groups:
alcohol, caffeine, sugar and fat.
—Alex Levine

Artists & Art Galleries

After 22 years in the education and corporate world, Annette Newbill Trujillo followed her passion for collecting contemporary art and fine craft into a successful gallery in her favorite town—Seaside! Newbill Collection by the Sea, 309 Ruskin Pl., is in a classical Tuscan architectural structure near the Seaside Chapel. Newbill offers a discriminating collection of art by nationally and regionally acclaimed artists. You'll find paintings, glass, ceramics, photography, and folk art for your home or office, an extensive selection of hand-crafted art jewelry, garden sculpture, and personal expressions for giving. Your shopping experience here will inspire, stimulate and challenge your senses. As Seaside's longest operating gallery, customers tell us over and over, "This is our favorite place to shop at Seaside." Newbill is open Monday-Saturday 11 am-5 pm and Sunday noon-5 pm. Call 850-231-4500. *(Color picture featured in front section of the book.)*

For more than 20 years Russ Gilbert has been doing something he loves—blowing glass. In 1995, he decided to share his extraordinary talent and this "American Art Glass" with Northwest Florida. Originality is what you will find at Fusion Art Glass, 63 Central Sq. This Seaside art gallery is itself an original. More than 200 other emerging and established artisans in the innovative craft of glass art join owner-and-operator Russ Gilbert in displaying their work. As Russ selects which artist's work to carry, he says he focuses on choosing the pieces that are whimsical or elegant. Every piece of art offers an amazing array of color. Unlike other genres of art, there are no prints in glass. Each piece is handmade, one at a time. Russ says that if you like original artwork, then glass is for you. As you stroll through the gallery, you will experience the pure, undefiled beauty of the multitude of creations. Anything the mind can imagine and beyond can be shaped from glass—custom jewelry, lighting, stemware, vases and sculpture—just to name a few.

Russ selects outstanding examples of each technique that is used in creating art glass. The different techniques include furnacework, flamework, fused, cast, slumped, sandblasted, coldwork, stained, reverse painting and mosaic. Since Russ is an accomplished flameworker, which is a "hot" technique, the majority of the glass he chooses for the gallery is made using molten glass with the flame, furnace and casting techniques. At Fusion Art Glass it's obvious they know glass. Gallery hours are 10 am-9 pm in the summer; 10 am-7 pm in the spring and fall; and 10 am-6 pm in the winter. Visit www.fusionartglass.com online or call 850-231-5405 to learn more. *(Color picture featured in front section of the book.)*

ESTABLISHED 1997

J. PROCTOR GALLERY

Seaside Florida

After a futile attempt at early retirement in New Orleans, Judith Proctor followed her heart back to Seaside to fulfill a dream-opening a fine art gallery. J. Proctor Gallery, 123 Quincy Cir. in Seaside was worth the wait. Surrounded by the things she lovesthe ocean, blue skies, seagulls, and beautiful paintings, Judith feels that her Seaside gallery is "just about perfect!" The bright blue French doors of the gallery open to the breathtaking views of the ocean, while inside, canvases from floor to ceiling display a compelling collection of watercolors, oils, acrylics, charcoals, and photography. The gallery represents artists from around the worldall Judith's favorites. Some of the most well-known artists include: abstract watercolorist Wilma Draper; photographer Michael Kahn; painter Jann Harrison; and more. Judith is also very proud to represent Donald Laurent Dahlke, one of the most prolifically diverse artists of this age, and Sergei Shillabeer, whose images capture the heart and mind of the viewer. Both novice and serious art lovers will find the perfect piece for their collection, with prices ranging from the low hundreds to thousands of dollars. The gallery opens daily at 10 am. Call 850-231-1091 or visit www.jproctorgallery.com online.

Bed and Breakfast

Josephine's was rated one of the top 12 inns in America and recently honored as one of the best romantic escapes in Florida by *Trend Magazine*. Set in the architecturally award-winning town of Seaside on the Gulf of Mexico, Josephine's awaits the weary traveler with many delights.

Owned and operated by Bruce and Judy Albert, you'll receive all of the warmth and charm of a family-run business with the comfort and privacy of a small luxury hotel. Josephine's breakfasts are renowned among its guests and outside diners alike. Seaside boasts excellent, eclectic shopping; world-class golf; sports; incredible dining; Josephine's cozy rooms; and some of the most beautiful beaches in the world.

Josephine's, 38 Seaside Ave., is also available for private parties, bridal luncheons, and family reunions. Visit online www.josephinesinn.com or call 800-848-1840.

IDYLL-BY-THE-SEA

Plan on "idyllic" days and nights in this incredibly beautiful and luxurious rental cottage called Idyll-By-The-Sea. Overlooking the charming town of Seaside at 2040 E. County Rd. 30A, the shingle-style cottage sports Bahama shutters; a "Tabby" or oyster shell fireplace; cut railing around the porch; and a sheep weathervane (because the owners have raised Cheviot sheep for 30 years!) The owners live and work in this beautiful cottage part of the year and rent it out the rest, so others can enjoy it! They have personally chosen every piece of wood, hardware, fabric, and wallpaper for the cottage, and some of the furniture has been in their family for generations. The dining table, for instance, was a great-grandmother's herb-drying table. And, the unique doorknobs were collected over many years. Outside, you'll find an evolving garden design. There are culinary herb beds and flowerbeds by the Gulf, and of course, a fig tree on one corner of the house, (something no old Southern cottage could be without!) For information, a brochure, or reservations, call 877-877-1102 or visit www.idyll-by-the-sea.com online.

At the heart of any memorable celebration is a great meal. Fancy Tomato has been the secret ingredient to successful celebrations all along the Emerald Coast since 1994. Owners Douglas and Patricia Alley (a.k.a. Chef Doug and Patti) offer full-service catering and design service in your home, office, or chosen venue. They furnish everything from a wide range of menu selections to exciting choices of fine linens, flowers, china and tablescapes. Fancy Tomato manages the details that make memories. The facilities are located at 55 Clayton Ln. in Grayton Beach, and include a private dining room perfect for small private parties. The Fancy Tomato has been voted "Best Catering Company on the Emerald Coast" by *Emerald Coast Magazine* for three consecutive years. *Birmingham Magazine* said, "Fanciful name. Fancy food. Fancy Tomato Catering brings great food right to great events and parties all over South Walton." And, Fancy Tomato is especially popular for exquisite customized wedding designs that have been featured in *Southern Living* magazine. The little business started by this husband-and-wife team has grown to employ seven full-time and 60 part-time partners. Visit www.fancytomato.com or call 850-231-0022.

In the beautiful and unique community of Seaside, life happens at a very casual pace. Generations spend the summer together on the beach from sunrise to sunset and lounge on the porches with cool drinks and gameboards. However your kiddos spend their time here, they will find the perfect clothing and accessories for a wonderful summer. This fun shop is located in Four Corners of the Merchants of Seaside at 2236 E. Co. Hwy. 30A, and is "just 4 kids!" You'll find beach fashions for infants, boys, and girls up to size 14. Kids love the fun beach toys for days in the sun, (we suspect that kids of "all ages" enjoy them,) and there are great games and toys for those rainy days back at the cottage. You'll find a large selection of bathing suits; cover-ups; flip-flops; and beachwear; as well as fun and colorful accessories. The shop is open daily 10 am-6 pm and until 9 pm Memorial Day-Labor Day. Call 850-231-1733.

If you're not familiar with the birth of Seaside, it is a charming story of family, tradition, and generational summer living. At least that was Robert Davis' inspiration for founding Seaside in 1981. Drawing upon his childhood memories of days spent wrapped in a towel on the front porch after a long day in the ocean, he and Daryl Davis chose the name "Seaside" for their remarkable little community.

The Seaside Store is the only purveyor of the "Seaside" brand, and the only store that sells Seaside logo merchandise—from the classic "NewTown" shirt to postcards depicting Steven Brooke's photography to T-shirts featuring local artists Woodie Long, Billie Gaffrey, Donna Burgess, Becky Ward and Cara Roy. Very cool, and very collectible! Open daily 10 am-6 pm and Memorial Day through Labor Day 10 am-9 pm. Call 850-231-2497 or visit www.theseasidestore.com.

When Dorothy Baratta opened Quincy, 122 Quincy Cir. in Seaside, she hoped to create a unique store that would be fun for the whole family. Mission accomplished! Her "Please Touch" displays encourage kids of all  ages to play—be sure to check out the wonderful art supplies, puppets and games. Call 850-231-0874 for art class schedule or visit www.quincyshop.com online. *(Color picture featured in front section of the book.)*

PERSPICASITY

Shop Barefoot by the Sea

All of the shops in Seaside are extremely unique and wonderful, but the genesis of the successful marketplace lies with Daryl Davis' venture into the world of retail—Perspicasity—a word meaning keenness of insight. While she and her husband Robert Davis the developer of Seaside, traveled through Italy and the Mediterranean, they had

always marveled at the open air, canvas-shaded markets that seemed to draw the entire community together to shop and visit. This was what she envisioned for Seaside. So, she set up displays of fresh fruit and vegetables, and soon had a variety of pioneering souls bring arts, crafts, and wonderful treasures to the "market" to sell. The trend soon caught on.

In the following years, she added eclectic cotton clothing, unique accessories, and fun gifts for the home. Daryl teamed with her good friend Mary Patton and the talented architect Deborah Berke and landscape designer Douglas Duany to create a courtyard of canvas awnings, resembling beach cabanas for the different huts. The atmosphere is charming. Shopping at Perspicasity, on the beachside in Seaside is a truly glorious experience. You will love browsing through this delightful store and finding the perfect reminder of your incredible visit to this idyllic community.

From linens to cotton—you'll find clothes you can live in, while looking stylish. Casual to chic—this store has got you covered! There is something for everyone. In fact, you may need to purchase an extra suitcase just to bring home all of your treasures! Perspicasity is open daily 10 am-6 pm and 10 am-9 pm Memorial Day through Labor Day. Call 850-231-5829 to learn more.

Cosmetics, Health & Beauty Products

patchouli's
Body, Bath & Home

Linda Boswell believes that different scents can make you happy, give you energy, or calm your mood. When she opened *patchouli's*, it was the only bath and body boutique between Tampa and New Orleans, and it has remained a favorite throughout northwest Florida for many years. Linda has filled her beautiful shop with precious items from around the world, and has designed her own line of custom-scented products. Customers love to browse and experiment with the different bath and body luxuries before they buy, so every product has a tester. Loyal *patchouli's* customers drive many miles to discover the newest trends in pamper products, or stock up on long-time favorites. There are special gifts for the bath and boudoir—perfect for girls who love to be pampered. Located at 45 Laura Hamilton Blvd., Santa Rosa Beach, in Gulf Place. Open daily, 10 am-9 pm in season, until 7 pm off-season, and until 6 pm in the winter. Call 850-231-1447 or www.patchoulis.com.

Restaurants

Florida Trend Magazine has been touting Criolla's as "One of Florida's Top 20 Restaurants" since 1991—with good reason! This incredible eatery at 170 E. Scenic Hwy. 30A is one of the first pioneer gourmet restaurants in the Destin area, as well as a full line catering and events planning company. Owner and chef Johnny Earles has drawn upon his Louisiana heritage, and his tutelage under world-renowned chefs, to develop a magnificent menu. The atmosphere is elegant and intimate with Caribbean decor, beautiful lighting, and crisp white linens. Join Debbie and Johnny Earles for an unforgettable dinner beginning at 5:30 pm, or let them cater your next special event. Visit their website, www.criollas.com online for seasonal hour changes and catering information. Call 850-267-1267.

Contemporary Italian

In a warm, intimate setting reminiscent of Italy's countryside, we found a small Italian restaurant with the body and substance of a classic "Trattoria." Mark E. Anton and Michael J. Dragon have partnered with Jaie T. O'Banner to bring contemporary Italian to Grayton Beach and the Emerald Coast. The robust, homemade food is the heart and soul of this restaurant, but the talented chefs have given classic Italian dishes a delicious twist. Be sure to try the Arroncini—a ball of risotto stuffed with mozzarella cheese, fried, then baked in the oven. In addition, try one of the two other favorites, the Grouper Nicoise—pan-seared grouper over whipped potatoes, artichokes, olives, and haricot verts and with a lemon white wine butter or the balsamic glazed pork tenderloin with stone ground polenta and sautéed spinach. You will appreciate the variety of wines available as well as the unpretentious atmosphere of Borago, 80 E. Hwy. 30A. And, you will *love* the food. Call 850-231-9167 for reservations or hours of operation, as they change seasonally. Please visit www.boragorestaurant.com online for the menu, wine list and directions.

BUD & ALLEY'S

RESTAURANT

Dave Rauschkolb and Scott Witcoski have been "riding the wave" of success for more than 18 years now, as their award-winning Seaside restaurant Bud & Alley's, 2236 E. Co. Hwy. 30A in Seaside, has grown into a beachfront mecca. The casual open-air dining and panoramic views of Seaside and the Gulf of Mexico create the perfect setting for comfortable, but very elegant dining. Ask any local, and you'll discover that Bud & Alley's is the place to be. The lively bands on the Roof Top Bar keep the beach hopping till the surfers come out; in fact, the surf is where Dave and Scott met, and where they say they hold their "board meetings!" The fresh seafood is wonderful, and the atmosphere perfect. Open daily 11:30 am-3 pm for lunch and 5:30-9:30 pm for dinner. (Closed during January and on Tuesdays in October, December and February.) Call 850-231-5900 or visit www.budandalleys.com online.

DISCOVER
MEXICO BEACH / PORT ST. JOE

MEXICO BEACH

Hidden Treasures

The history of Mexico Beach is filled with mystery and intrigue. Whispers of Caribbean Pirates from the 1800s and their grand stashes of stolen treasures yet to be discovered lure you into the many inland hideaways. In 1920, the Florida Department of Transportation built the Scenic U.S. Hwy. 98. It was at this time that a gentleman named Felix DuPont purchased the land now known as Mexico Beach for the purpose of turpentine farming.

Nestled between Cape San Blas to the east, and Panama City to the west, Mexico Beach is a favorite spot for thousands of vacationers each year. It has become a "Mecca" for anglers. They come for offshore adventure or relaxing surf fishing, but at the end of the day, they walk away with much more than just a cooler full of fish. They have experienced the captivating warmth and the magical enchantment of this hidden part of "Old Florida."

Mexico Beach has been called "The Quiet Alternative, a peaceful hamlet that has remained untouched by commercialism." It offers charming simplicity with its beautiful white beaches, and no high-rises to block the views of the incredible sunsets. There are no crowds, no traffic, no fast food chains—nothing to distract from the natural, quiet beauty of this coastal paradise. You will awaken not to the sounds of honking horns or screeching tires, but to the soft sounds of waves lapping over sugar white beaches and the whispering of palms rustling in the Gulf breezes. It is a place where the most important decision of the day is whether to spend the day shopping, laze on the beach or try your pole at fishing. And, it is a place where locals and vacationers are treated in the same friendly manner. The waters are some of the safest on the Gulf Coast, with large sandbars protecting the swimming areas, so that children can "chase the surf" to their hearts' content. The beach is not only a private sanctuary for people, but also a place where even the birds find peace. Bring your binoculars for sightings of many rare species, as well as the comical pelicans and the famed "osprey" which make their home here.

The people of Mexico Beach would prefer; however, that you not tell too many people about their Forgotten Beach. They love the unspoiled simplicity as much as you will, and ask that you keep its location as a secret hideout for you and your loved ones. Unlike other resort areas, this is a place for rejuvenation—a place where families can share time and make memories. Its beautiful tranquility will stay with you forever. We can't be certain where the pirates hid their treasure, but we do know that Mexico Beach is indeed a treasure all its own. Visit Mexico Beach to rejuvenate your senses, spirit, and emotions. The gentle shores await.

Angling Opportunities

Whether you are after "the big one" off shore, or prefer to spend hours watching your cork bobble on the water, you will love the fishing opportunities that abound in Mexico Beach. Drop your line off the City Pier, or try your rod and reel in the beach surf, but get the ice chest ready, because you'll probably go home with dinner—red fish, trout, flounder, or a trap full of blue crabs! For deep-water fishing, Mexico Beach has many fine professionals whose charter boat excursions provide a lifetime of "fish tales!" Schedule a four, six, or even eight hour in-shore trolling trip for kings, Spanish, blues, blue dolphin, tuna, ling or cobia, or a longer trip for grouper and snapper. Be sure to ask your charter boat captain about the many tournaments throughout the year. Charters are available for both off shore or in shore fishing, or exciting scuba diving excursions. (Mayhap you'll find the hidden treasure!)

PORT ST. JOE

Take off your fancy timepieces; dig your toes in the sand; and enjoy this little part of paradise that is one of Florida's best-kept secrets. Incredibly rich in culture and beauty, Port St. Joe boasts wonderful fresh and saltwater fishing, pristine white (uncrowded) beaches, and a laid-back atmosphere that charms and captivates. It is part of what is known as "Old Florida," or the "Forgotten Coast," and is a jewel of a place almost suspended in time. Port St. Joe natives enjoy life at a gentle pace, where 56 American flags line the main street, and where most people "go fishin'" every Friday. Everyone in town knows everyone in town—by first names! This idyllic, beautiful town is like a "step back in time." It's a place where you can slow down and enjoy the giggles and wonder of your children as they explore the beach. It has been said that Port St. Joe is "a place where folks still think it's important to take their kids to Sunday School, and to measure their success by their quality of life," or that a visit is like "stepping into a Norman Rockwell painting." We'd have to agree!

Downtown Charm—Charming Shopping

This quaint, picturesque area of the Forgotten Coast is the largest city of Gulf County and the county seat. It lives in the history books because it was here, in 1838, that delegates from all counties in Florida assembled to draft Florida's first State Constitution. The Constitution Monument Park was erected in 1922 and bears the names of the delegates engraved in marble. It is one of the most beautiful parks in Gulf County, perfect for concerts, social gatherings, and weddings. History buffs, don't miss a tour of the historical Port St. Joe Cemetery, which is a grim reminder of this town's virtual annihilation by yellow fever and a hurricane in 1844.

The downtown area has been transformed into a charming strolling, browsing, and shopping area that provides a wonderful diversion from "fun in the sun." You'll find everything here except the hustle and bustle, traffic lights, and crowds of strangers. In fact, no one stays a stranger long around here. You'll find that when someone asks, "How are you doing," they really want to know! It's small town atmosphere and friendly people are Port St. Joe's most important attribute. You can visit antique galleries and auction houses where you'll find everything from fine furniture to dollar treasures. You'll love the jewelry, coins, and art. From the mom and pop restaurants and bakeries, to the fruit and produce stands and seafood markets—visitors truly get an authentic taste of this delightful coastal community.

Get Out—Outside That Is!

After all, that's why you're here! Port St. Joe beaches are known for their crystal sapphire waters, incredibly white beaches, and striking sunsets. Here, the emphasis is on "family." The beach is rated one of the safest in Florida because of the barrier island. With very little undertow, the waters are safe enough that children swim and explore safely; float or "ride the waves;" or conquer the water by kayak. St. Joe Beaches offer visitors seclusion and privacy, as well as opportunities to crab, scallop, or search for shells. The recreational scallop season is always July 1 through September 10. Maybe you'll even get the chance to witness a sea turtle laying its eggs at moonlight. Families come together in this unhurried, slow-paced community to discover God's wonderful creation, and to rediscover in each other the things that make them family.

For more information on Mexico Beach, call the Community Development Council at 888-723-2546 or 850-648-8196 or visit www.mexicobeach.com/cdc.

Visit www.gulfcountychamberofcommerce.com for more information on Port St. Joe, or call the Gulf County Chamber of Commerce at 800-239-9553 or 850-237-1223. Or, call the Gulf County Tourist Development Council at 800-482-GULF (4853) or visit www.visitgulf.com.

**Mexico Beach / Port St. Joe
Fairs Festivals & Fun**

January
>Living History Day

February
>Charity Mardi Gras Gala
>Annual Mexico Beach Gumbo Cookoff

April
>Antique Car Show
>Annual Mexico Beach Photography Contest
>Annual Mexico Beach Ling Tournament & Festival

May
>Port St. Joe Marina Spring Fishing Tournament
>Tupelo Honey Festival

June
>Port St. Joe "Kid's Win" Fishing Tournament
>Big Bend Fishing Tournament
>Dockside/GALA Classic Fishing Tournament

July
>Port St. Joe Independence Day Summer Celebration
>Redfish Tournament at the Port St. Joe Marina
>Mexico Beach Independence Celebration

August
>Wewahitchka Catfish Classic Festival & Fishing Tournament
>Mexico Beach Annual Kingfish Tournament

September
>Port St. Joe Scallop Festival-Labor Day Weekend

October
>Monumental Music
>Florida Panhandle Birding & Wildflower Festival
>Annual Mexico Beach Art & Wine Festival
>Mexico Beach "Haunted House & Carnival"
>Port St. Joe's "Ghosts on the Coast" Celebration

December
>Port St. Joe "Christmas on the Coast" Celebration
>Mexico Beach Christmas Celebration of Lights
>Beaches New Year's Eve Celebration

Donna Spears Realty
& VACATION RENTALS

Donna Spears loves to quote her mother who always said: "Go first class, or stay home!" She understands now that her mother wasn't just talking about travel, but also about day-to-day life. She is also proud that her entire realty staff shares this philosophy of "not cutting corners." They do everything it takes to get the job done right. Reared in Port St. Joe, Donna has many years of experience in the Gulf County area. Her specialty is beach property from Indian Pass to Cape San Blas. In just three short years, she became one of the top-producing agents in the state of Florida, and is an annual multi-million dollar producer. She is also one of the friendliest, most hardworking individuals you will ever meet. Donna says she "sells sand and sandcastles," and will help you find the property that is right for you at the right price. Her commitment to helping her clients make their dreams come true is evident from the first hello to the final handshake. Stop by Donna Spears Realty at 6335-C Hwy. 30A in Port St. Joe. Hours are 8:30 am-5:30 pm Monday-Saturday and 1-5 pm Sunday. For more information, visit www.donnaspearsrealty.com or call 850-227-7879, 800-293-0428.

The beautiful Mexico Beach and Cape San Blas area makes up the majority of Florida's "Forgotten Coast." This is a thriving community, whose best assets are its friendly people; its preserved natural beauty; and its ability to remain one of the few uncrowded and uncommercialized beaches. Visitors delight in the sugar-white sands and blue-green waters—perfect for sunbathing, shelling, and water sports. The intracoastal waterway and its myriad of rivers, creeks, and lakes are a fisherman's paradise, and its 2,500-acre wildlife refuge is a haven for bird and wildlife enthusiasts. There are annual Kingfish and Ling Fish tournaments; festivals for bay oystering, scalloping and crabbing; and marinas with boat rentals and fishing charters.

If this sounds just about perfect for your next family vacation, let Coldwell Banker Forgotten Coast Realty, 710 Hwy. 98 in Mexico Beach, make it a reality. Coldwell Banker has been providing full service real estate for more than 94 years, and is a first choice for vacation rentals along the coast. Coldwell's professional property management team and vacation specialists are available for vacation planning, or helping you find a place to settle for a lifetime. Choose from beachfront, canal front, or Gulf view, in either condominiums, townhomes, or single-family homes. The Forgotten Coast remains a treasure to all who visit—a feast for the eyes, senses, spirit, and emotions. Trust Coldwell Banker Forgotten Coast Realty to help make your vacation dream come true. Office hours are Monday-Saturday 9 am-5:30 pm and Sunday 10 am-4 pm. Call 850-648-1011, 866-648-1011 or visit www.cbforgottencoast.com online. Each office is independently owned and operated.

Turtle Beach Inn

Nestled between long-needled pines and cabbage palms on the Gulf, Turtle Beach Inn and Cottages seems almost lost in time. This part of Florida features unspoiled Gulf sands and sea, and a visit to Turtle Beach offers balmy beachfront porches and pure relaxation. Choose from rooms at Turtle Beach Inn, Turtle Tower, or the Sand Dollar Cottage—all absolutely charming and cozy! The outside porches, both upstairs and down, overlook the Gulf of Mexico. The inn also manages nearby privately-owned rental cottages. Visit www.turtlebeachinn.com for a virtual tour of this wonderful inn; call 850-229-9366; or stop by 140 Painted Pony Rd in Port St. Joe.

The Four Stages of Life

You believe in Santa Clause.

You don't believe in Santa Clause.

You are Santa Clause.

You look Like Santa Clause.

—Unknown

Gifts, Home Décor, Gourmet & Specialty Foods

Prickly Pears

Gourmet Gallery

Gourmet Food + Chocolate + Art + Wine + Cheese = Prickly Pears Gourmet Gallery, on the corner of Hwy. 98 and 36th St. in Mexico Beach. The brightly-painted walls and the wonderful smell of fresh spices give this charming shop a tropical feel. In fact, it has been referred to as "the most colorful shop on the beach." You'll find a wide variety of specialty foods including gourmet chocolates, cheeses, coffees, teas, imported foods, organic spices, and a wonderful variety of wine, plus gifts and kitchenware. Custom gift baskets are available for any occasion. Samplings of dozens of gourmet goodies are always to be had at the tasting table as you enter the store. Dolores Lowery has always loved to cook, but couldn't find the specialty items she needed in the area. Being an art lover, her idea evolved into a "Gourmet Gallery" with exhibits by local artists. The result is a wonderful combination—Fabulous Food + Awesome Art = Great Fun! You can even schedule cooking classes for up to six people. Open Tuesday-Saturday 10 am-6 pm. Call 850-648-1115 or visit www.pricklypears.net.

From candles to sailboats, and teapots to trellises, if you browse long enough, you will probably find it here. This amazing store at 328 Reid Ave. in Port St. Joe, has the feel and definitely the name of a "general store," but the similarities stop there. It is a very unique shop filled with everything you can imagine for the home, garden, or beach house along with personal items too—check out the Italian 18k charm bracelets!

The showroom is a wide open space of more than 3,500 square feet, filled with exciting items such as prints and framed art; bath accessories; fringed lamps; pillows and throws; colorful household furnishings; antiques; nautical items and even the aromatic Trapp candles. Owners Marie and Tom Todd are very excited that their eclectic shop draws customers from far and near. Stop by! Open Monday-Saturday 10 am-5 pm. Call 850-227-1950.

Success at age:

4 – not peeing in your pants

12 – having friends

16 – having a drivers license

20 – going all the way

35 – having money

50 – having money

60 – going all the way

70 – having a drivers license

75 – having friends

80 – not peeing in your pants

—Unknown

Cafés & Restaurants

Beautiful St. Joe Bay and Cape San Blas provide the breath-taking view for a dining experience that stands out among the best. Dockside Café, at 342 W. 1st St. in Port St. Joe, is well-known throughout the area for its prize-winning seafood dishes. Glen Singleton and wife Charlotte combine talents and creative ideas in preparing some of the most delicious meals you will ever enjoy including packed lunches for a day out on the Gulf!

They receive rave reviews about their Seafood Gumbo, and their recipe for Fried Shrimp has been featured as a "*Southern Living* Favorite.*" They also have a fresh seafood market and will vacuum

pack your purchase for travel. Fishermen may take advantage of the bait shack for live or frozen baits. The deck is enclosed and heated for outdoor dining.

Open 11 am-9 pm Monday-Thursday, until 10 pm Friday and Saturday and until 4 pm Sunday. Call 850-229-5200.

Owner and Chef Kathy Whittemore describes her charming café as "a touch of Europe with the flavor of the Gulf." The menu includes wonderful soups; salads; sandwiches; pastas; chicken and seafood. Her signature dish is a delicious grouper stuffed with crab, encrusted in breadcrumbs and nuts, and topped with smoked Havarti cheese! You'll love her dessert selections, too. Kathy is well-known as one of the premiere caterers in the Bay, Gulf, and Franklin counties. We found old Florida-style friendliness, a relaxing atmosphere and superb food. Stop by for a glass of wine and appetizers, or wine with fresh desserts for the close of an evening. Beluga Café—the only patio-dining in town—108 1st St. in Port St. Joe, is open Monday-Wednesday 11 am-4 pm; Thursday-Friday until 8 pm; Saturday with live music until 10 pm; and Sunday 10 am-2 pm. Call 850-227-3500 or visit www.belugacafe.net.

Rock, Head On, Large, Jumbo, or Monster—you choose the type of shrimp you want and whether you like yours mild or spicy. Then, sit back and get ready to enjoy an incredible seafood treat. Jay Jay Ray and the staff at Half Shells know how to steam seafood to perfection. The Ray family has been in the seafood business, both commercially and recreationally, for three generations. The Rays' popular restaurant, Half Shells, at 3104 Hwy. 98 in Mexico Beach, is known for the large selection of fresh seafood cooked "just the way you want it," as well as for its fun, casual, and nautical atmosphere. Half Shells has been featured in *Southern Living Magazine*, the *Albany Journal*, and the *Atlanta Journal-Constitution*. It is great food and great fun! Hours are Sunday-Thursday 10 am-9 pm and Friday-Saturday until 10 pm. For more information, visit www.halfshells.com or 850-648-2000.

DISCOVER
NICEVILLE / VALPARAISO

Those lucky enough to live in Florida's beautiful bay area know that they are the envy of many. They know that they live in paradise, and so they focus on enjoying every minute and inch of it! Whether you are visiting for a day, a week, or longer, you will immediately feel the warmth and sincerity of the people throughout Niceville and Valparaiso. These bay cities are relatively young, with city charters granted as late as 1921 and 1938. The draw to the bay area, aside from the tranquil beauty of the place, was the timberlands. The straight pine heartwood was in great demand throughout the entire world—mostly for furniture and homes.

A Fisherwoman's Paradise

Equally as important as the timber, were the navigable waterways and access to the seas—both important for transportation and industry. Today, fishing is a leading industry for the area. In fact, it has been called a "virtual fisherman's paradise." There are freshwater lakes; ponds and streams brimming with bass and catfish; and bay waters filled with flounder, red fish, trout, shrimp, and oysters. If you dare venture out into the deep waters for the bigger catches of snapper, tarpon, marlin, or sailfish—saltwater fishing is available through several charter services.

Twin City Activities

The fishing is great; the sunsets are beautiful; and the food is fabulous. But if you want to really get a taste of the true flavor of the Bay Area, look to the museums and city parks, as well as the annual festivals that celebrate the passion and style of the locals. From "Saturdays in the Park" in the spring to "Yule of Yesteryear in December," there is always a reason to celebrate. Another great way to absorb the history of the Bay Area? Visit The Heritage Museum of Northwest Florida. Learn the story from prehistoric times through the 20th century. Who would have dreamed that history could be such fun?

The Boggy Bayou Mullet Festival is one of the largest in the Northwest Florida region. The three-day event highlights the arts, crafts, and food, with non-stop entertainment featuring well-known performing personalities.

For more information on Niceville and Valparaiso, contact the Niceville-Valparaiso-Bay Area Chamber of Commerce at 850-678-2323 or visit www.nicevillechamber.com online.

Niceville / Valparaiso Fairs Festivals & Fun

April
>   Saturday in the Park Arts & Crafts Festival
>   Easter Egg Dash

July
>   Fireworks

September
>   Mid-Bay Bridge Run/Walk

October
>   Boggy Bayou Mullet Festival
>   Oktoberfest

December
>   Christmas Parade
>   Yule of Yesteryear

Antiques, Artists
Art Galleries & Interior Design

jd INTERIORS

A personal touch is what jd Interiors, 1016 John Sims Pkwy., Niceville, has to offer its cliental. Jan Strunk, the owner and licensed interior decorator, has been in the design business for more than 25 years. She has worked with people from many

different cultures—both stateside and abroad. Whether it's simply a wonderful lamp to fit your den or an array of unique accessories for the home, you'll be satisfied with the heartfelt help and quality of jd Interiors. As a child, Jan had a passion for arranging furniture and making things look pretty. That passion continues, and her associates at jd Interiors share this passion and love of design. They especially take great joy in working closely with people as they design their classic and timeless interiors. Jan says they truly believe in designing rooms that reflect the people who live there. Retail showroom hours are Monday-Friday 9 am-5 pm. Call 850-729-7688.

PIED PIFFLE

The name absolutely fits owner Jean Ruckel, and her eclectic A-frame at 274 Edge Ave. in Valparaiso. A white picket fence frames this darling cottage that doubles as her shop and home, and her garden grows and changes daily. Pied Piffle (pronounced apple pie PIED, and PIFFLE that rhymes with whiffle, means "colorful nonsense,") perfectly describes the collection of shabby chic. Iron furniture, antiques—fine and casual—linens, and paintings, fill every corner of the store. Jean is an artist with a "bohemian soul," whose paintings are both whimsical and formal. You truly must see this shop to believe it. Open Wednesday-Saturday 10 am-4:30 pm. Call 850-678-1734. *(Color picture featured in front section of the book.)*

POLLY'S CONCRETE PRODUCTS, INC.

Since taking over her late father's business in 1993, Sherrie Venghaus has grown Polly's Concrete Products at 4619 Hwy. 20 in Niceville into one of the best sources for landscape enhancement on the Emerald Coast. Polly's has more than 1,000 molds! Sherrie, and her husband Mike, have expanded the business to include driveway and patio concrete installation or repair, and more! Hours are Monday-Saturday 8 am-4 pm. Be sure to call 850-897-3314 or to visit www.pollysconcrete.com.

Bayou Book Company

Hallmark

In a time when giant conglomerates devour small, family-owned businesses, it is so refreshing to see a town support wonderful places like the Bayou Book Company. When the Chessers opened the store at 1118 John Sims Pkwy. in Niceville in 1986, it was only 2,000 square feet, and they only carried books. They have now expanded to more than 6,000 square feet, and feature wonderful gifts, home décor, and Hallmark greeting cards. In fact, Bayou Book Company is now a "Gold Crown Store," quite an accomplishment for a lawyer and a music major/mother of four! Carolyn Chesser attributes much of their wonderful success to her great staff.

"My employees have a strong allegiance to the store and to each other," she says. "Several of them have been on board since its inception, and are all active community members." Someone very friendly and helpful is always ready to help with a selection or suggestion, and the store's inventory of books changes often. Another factor in the store's growth has been its involvement in the community. Bayou Book Co. works with the local library on programs for the public, holding story times, cooking demonstrations, contests, author signings, and other various events. Look for the book sale cart outside, and the wonderful gifts in the window of this charming bookstore. You will appreciate the many differences in shopping this hometown, family-owned bookstore as opposed to a chain business where you are just a number. Bayou Book Co. is open Monday-Saturday 9 am - 7 pm, and Sunday (September-December) noon-5 pm. Call 850-678-1593 to learn more.

GILMORE
JEWELRY Co.

Bill and Susie Houck believe that, "Your Best Buy is With Your Hometown Jeweler Who Cares," and they have grown their successful business by earning the trust and confidence of their loyal customers. Gilmore Jewelry Company is a 29-year-old tradition, located in the Palm Plaza at 1023 John Sims Pkwy. in Niceville.

You will find two very beautiful designer lines of jewelry, including Ziva—high-end platinum, diamond and precious stones company, and Frank Reubel—high-end, semi-precious, contemporary line. In addition to the exquisite jewelry, Gilmore Jewelry Company offers excellent jewelry and watch repair services. For custom jewelry, just bring in a picture and they will create your dream! They will buy old gold and diamonds. The store is open Monday-Friday 9 am-5:30 pm and Saturday until 4 pm. Call 850-678-1411.

Restaurants

Accessible by car or boat, this terrific waterfront restaurant provides a beautiful sunset view, as well as delicious seafood, steaks and pasta. Giuseppi's Wharf is tucked away at 821 Bayshore Dr. in Niceville, overlooking beautiful Boggy Bayou. Visit Giuseppi's other location at 1176 N. Eglin Pkwy. in Shalimar. Giuseppi's offers locals and visitors indoor dining, outdoor decks overlooking the marina, and a beautiful shaded area "Down-under" for special events. The atmosphere is very "beachy" and friendly, so dress casually, but bring a big appetite! Musical entertainment is provided on the Tiki Hut deck, which can seat 150 people. The marina includes 50 boat slips

for water travelers. Come early so you can watch the sun go down over the bayou and enjoy the delicious creations from the sea. Hours are daily 11 am to 10 pm. Visit online at www.giuseppiswharf.com or call 850-678-4229 for more information.

The Leaf n' Ladle Restaurant and Catering

For "food done right at a reasonable price" it's the Leaf N' Ladle. Open Monday-Friday, 11 am-2 pm, check out the buffet featuring two hot entrees, two homemade soups, and a full array of fresh veggies, salads, and breads. Or, choose from a full service menu and, don't forget dessert—the cheesecakes and bread pudding are unforgettable! The Leaf N' Ladle has been in operation since 1982 at 137 S. John Sims Pkwy. in Valparasio—a testimony to its excellence. Call 850-678-3504 or visit www.leafnladle.com.

THE BOATHOUSE LANDING RESTAURANT

You will love this charming waterfront seafood restaurant at 124 John Sims Pkwy. in Valparasio. The Boathouse Landing offers incredible seafood such as grilled red snapper, fried shrimp, garlic-crusted grouper, delicious Seafood Gumbo, and of course, great views of the bayou and boats. A small dock with boat slips provides access by water to The Boathouse Landing. Discover what the locals already know! The restaurant is open daily for lunch and dinner. Call 850-678-2805.

There is no descent meal without dessert.

Ashley Adams, Age 11

DISCOVER PANAMA CITY BEACH

Panama City Beach has earned quite a few nicknames through the years, including "Best Beach in America;" " Best Sports Beach on the Gulf;" "Wreck Capital of the South;" and "Seafood Capital of the World." All of these are fitting, but we think you'll find your own special words for this family-friendly, action-packed, very cool part of the beautiful Emerald Coast. Locals are most proud of the latest award, "#4 Best Beach in America!" There are 27 miles of snowy white sand and crystal blue–green water, so lather on the sunscreen and enjoy! Explore the hundreds of miles of Gulf waters, as well as bays, bayous, and lakes. You'll find many opportunities to build new family memories. Don't be surprised to find that everyone will want to get up early so they don't miss one minute of adventure. Whether you are traveling with a large family; just with a "loved one;" or even with a few ladies on a "Day Out;" you will find the relaxed way of life here in Panama City Beach, and the charm and friendliness of the people, will make your visit unforgettable.

Fun In the Sun

You will be amazed at the number of adventures in store for you in Panama City Beach. Of course, if you want to . . . you can soak in the sun with a good book; build a sandcastle; laugh with the dolphins; enjoy a wonderful dinner; delight in a crimson sunset; and then . . . start all over again tomorrow. However, the more adventurous can set sail on one of the multi-colored sailboats skimming across the Gulf, or rent a windsurfer or Jet Ski. Charter companies abound here, ready to lift anchor for a snorkeling and shelling excursion; an exploration of the ocean floor from a glass bottom boat; a sunset dinner cruise and more.

If you are wondering about the nickname, "Wreck Capital of the South," don a wet suit and join a group of divers investigating the 50 artificial reefs and some of the many sunken vessels close to shore. From the tugboat Simpson (in only 25 feet of water) to The Empire Mica, which sunk in 192 feet of water when it was torpedoed in 1942 by a German U-boat, you can explore as long as your tank holds out. More timid snorkelers will love poking around the St. Andrews State Park jetties, which have very shallow water, and no boat traffic. Here you'll find an old tar barge, only 19 feet under the surface.

There truly is something exciting for every age. From beach volleyball and hot dogs on the beach to searching the tide for keepsake shells, kids and "kids at heart" will love Panama City Beach!

Something For Everyone

Around the last cool days of winter, when the weather seems to warm just a bit, and the calendar turns the page to March, college coeds across the nation begin to daydream of that annual escape from exams and studying—the infamous "Spring Break." Students travel from across the southernmost parts of the United States for a "week in the sun," and Panama City Beach is usually one of their first choices. The entire beach comes to life with youthful exuberance during the month of March, and for this time; the beach belongs to the young. As soon as they head back to school though, the city opens her arms to another group—amilies and couples. This is a perfect romantic getaway for a weekend, week, or forever! You can take advantage of all of the first-class dining experiences, fun festivals, and the romantic sunsets. Many brides choose Panama City as a destination for a beach wedding—some at the water's edge, some under a beach canopy at evening, and some, believe it or not, *underwater*! Panama City Beach welcomes one and all to be her guest, to explore her many natural wonders, and to take home a treasured memory. One of the city's most endearing assets is her people. They are extremely friendly, welcoming to visitors, and of course, love where they live. Even the crusty "old salt" at the end of the fishing pier will share information, advice, and even his favorite fishing hole with a stranger. You will absolutely fall in love with this very "hip," yet laid-back Southern city. There is so much to do, and there is nothing to do, so pull up a beach chair and stay awhile.

For more information on Panama City Beach, call the Panama City Beach Convention and Visitor's Bureau at 800-PCBEACH or 850-233-6503 or visit www.800pcbeach.com.

March
Scottish Heritage Festival
Annual Azalea Trail
St. Patrick's Day Street Festival
Celebrate Downtown Arts & Antique Open House
Gulf Coast Salute – Air Show

April
Mr. Surf's Annual Zap Pro/Am Skim Jam
St. Andrews Shrimp Oyster Festival
Cobia Tournament
Gulf Coast Charity Walking Horse Show & Music Festival
Gulf Coast Spring Triathlon Series I

May
Annual Thunderbeach Motorcycle Rally
"Spring Festival of the Arts"
Touchstone Energy Southeastern Balloon Festival
Cinco de Mayo Festival
Gulf Coast Spring Triathlon Series II

June
Junior Anglers Fishing Rodeo
Kid's Fishing Clinic

July
   4th of July Fireworks/Celebration
   Bay Point Invitational Billfish Tournament
August
   Annual Faces and Facets
September
   Gulf Coast Sprint Triathlon Series III
   Annual King Mackerel Tournament
   Doll Club Annual Doll Show & Sale
   Corvette Beach Odyssey
   Lobster Festival & Tournament
   Annual Endless Summer Soccer Tournament
   Thunder Beach Autumn Motorcycle Rally
   St. Andrews Fall Seafood & Pirate Fest
   Bay Culinary Classic

October
   Gulf Coast Sprint Triathlon Series IV
   Nature's Gallery
   Central Panhandle Fair
   Octoberfest
   Deep Sea Fishing Rodeo
   Annual Indian Summer Festival
   March of Dimes Harvest Wine Festival
   Haunted Trail and Pumpkin Patch

November
   Celebrate Downtown & Festival of Nations
   Ironman Florida
   Holly Fair
   Panama City Garden Club Annual Bazaar
   Annual Bay Art Show
   Annual Greek Bake Sale

December
   Panama City Beach Christmas Parade
   The Christmas Tour of Homes
   Panama City Christmas Parade
   Annual Boat Parade of Lights

SCAVENGERS BAZAAR

Antiques and Interiors Market

Scavengers Bazaar, 532 N. Lakeshore Dr. in Panama City Beach, is an antique lover's dream, offering 7,500-square-feet of treasures. From inexpensive finds—a seashell—to high-end finds—a turn-of-the-century French armoire, this store has it all! Scavengers Bazaar has an eclectic mix of more than 60 dealers offering a wonderful variety of antiques and art. The owners are artists in their own right—creating a great selection of signed pieces of distressed and painted furniture.

You will be greeted at the front door by "Lucy" wearing nothing but her finest pearls—don't worry, she's just a prissy pup. And, while you are searching for your treasures, you can sing-a-long or even dance to your favorite oldies. This will be a shopping spree you won't soon forget. Stop by Monday-Saturday 10 am-5 pm and Sunday 1-5 pm. For more information, call 850-235-8095.

Panama City Beach
Fabric Factory

Simply charming, quaintly cozy, quite affordable and one-of-a-kind, are just a few phrases that perfectly describe this unique decorator store. Panama City Beach Fabric Factory at 12127 Panama City Beach Pkwy. carries wonderful decorator fabrics; trims and tassels; beaded trims; ready-to-decorate lampshades; home accents; and exciting gift items. You can also browse through a library of the latest fabric selections available to order. Owner Denise Freeman asks, "Why should good taste have to cost more?" Be sure to look for her husband's pottery throughout the store. Hours are 10 am-4 pm Tuesday-Saturday. Call 850-249-9090 or visit www.fabric-factory.com.

Consignment Gallery

Soon after neighbors Joyce Muller and Joyce Watts became friends, they realized they had a lot more in common than just a first name. Both Joyces had a love for decorating and a vision for what is now a beautifully original consignment shop in Panama City Beach.

Consignment Gallery, 8317 Front Beach Rd., brings a breath of fresh air to homes with its "gently used home furnishings and accessories." Each piece is carefully examined to help ensure quality purchases and satisfied customers. You're sure to find a special piece for your décor.

Housed in a signature Floridian style promenade mall, the shop also holds such unique items as screens, picture frames and unique accessories that will make your home come to life! Stop by Consignment Gallery to see what treasures the Joyces have in store for your home.

For more information, call 850-236-1892. Consignment Gallery is open Tuesday-Friday 10 am-4 pm and Saturday 10 am-1 pm.

Lady Anderson

DINING YACHT

For a truly unique dining experience, you may want to head out to sea. The Lady Anderson Dining Yacht harbored at 5550 N. Lagoon Dr. in Panama City Beach is a third-generation family business that takes eating out to a whole new level.

The Lady Anderson—named in honor of Capt. Max Anderson's wife—casually cruises around the St. Andrew Bay while her guests enjoy fine dining in the enclosed dining room or seated out in the open-air.

While gazing at the sparkling stars, guests can dance to the live music provided, or choose a cruise to sit back and listen to the sounds of the Gospel band drift over the ocean waters. For more information and hours of operation, call 850-234-5940 or visit online at www.ladyanderson.com.

Wild Dolphin Experience

For thousands of years, mankind has had a special connection with dolphins —as fascinated with them as they are with us. For Francisco Hidalgo, his passion for these magical beings began when he was a little boy watching "Flipper" in his "world full of wonder." After his first up-close-and-personal experience with dolphins, he knew exactly what he wanted to do with his life. Today, he offers the "Wild Dolphin Experience" for everyone, a unique opportunity to connect with the loving and playful bottlenose dolphins of Panama City Beach. You may take a daily excursion to swim with the dolphins in their natural habitat, as well as listen to their language as

they interact with their visitors. Because these groups are kept small, everyone is allowed to actually get into the water as much as possible. The crystal clear water is ideal for viewing and photographing the dolphins as you see them display their wonderfully exuberant and joyful nature. For information on Francisco's Wild Dolphin Experience, visit www.wilddolphinexperience.com or call 850-233-8771.

Spend your days on magnificent powder-white beaches; then kick back and relax at one of Sterling Resorts' luxury gulf-front condominiums in Panama City Beach or Destin. All four of Sterling's fabulous vacation retreats: Sterling Shores; Sterling Sands; Seafarer Condominiums; and Sterling Beach; offer unsurpassed "Sterling Plus" service. Located at 6627 Thomas Dr. in Panama City Beach, Sterling Beach features deluxe two-and-three bedroom condominiums with private balconies, fully equipped kitchens, and more! Families rave about the fabulous "movie nights" in the 48-seat surround sound theater. Enjoy a complimentary Starbucks coffee starter kit; special rates at nearby golf courses; bicycles and beach accessory rentals; and the daily newspaper. For more information or reservations, call 877-563-9595, 850-236-9595, or visit online at www.SterlingBeach.com or www.SterlingResorts.com.

Located in the heart of Panama City, the Americana Beach Motel is the place for family fun in the sun. Within walking distance of shopping, restaurants, grocery stores and amusement parks, this motel has been a number one pick for returning visitors for more than 25 years. However, once there, you may never want to leave the property! It's that great!

Each room is well equipped with the basic amenities and more! Family units are available with full-size kitchens and enough room to accommodate any size family. Step out your back door and play all day in the gulf-side heated pool or the crystal-blue waters of the Gulf of Mexico. Why not indulge in exciting water activities such as: parasailing, jet skiing or swimming? Or, if you'd rather relax, check out the beach chair rental service and catch some rays. Or better yet, join in a family game of beach volleyball. Then enjoy the dramatic and beautiful sunset from your private porch or balcony.

The Americana Beach Motel, 11807 Front Beach Rd., has been family-owned-and-operated since 1975. Not only is it still family run, but also it continues to be a favorite vacation spot for returning families and couples year after year. The Americana is the perfect location for special annual events as well!

Let the Americana Beach Motel give you the perfect getaway with its friendly service, sparkling clean facilities and breathtaking view. It's paradise—Florida style.

Open daily 8 am-10 pm and 7 am-midnight Memorial Day weekend through Labor Day weekend. For more information and reservations, visit www.americanamotel.com online or call 888-595-2275, 850-234-2275.

Motel & Tower

When the owner of Flamingo Motel and Tower says that you may come to Flamingo as a guest, but you will leave a friend, he is right. The Flamingo Motel and Tower, 15525 Front Beach Rd. in Panama City Beach, is a family-operated business with a family appearance. The Lancaster family started with 44 units on the beachfront property and now has 103 units. The motel was extensively remodeled in 1996, transforming it into a tropical garden paradise, and the Tower was built in 1998. The Lancasters have five daughters, which makes it easy to have at least one of the family members on property at all times. The Flamingo enjoys one of the most successful hotel operations on the Gulf Coast.

Regardless of your budget, the Flamingo Motel and Tower has the perfect room for you with 13 different room choices—from a room with one queen-size bed and a full kitchen to the Penthouse Suite with two bedrooms, a living room, a dining room, a full kitchen, a kids hide-away, two full baths and garden and gulf views. All rooms have microwaves and refrigerators and most rooms have full kitchens. And, all rooms are very clean. This beachfront property also includes large sundecks, two heated pools, and a heated spa.

It is the Lancasters sincere desire to provide a happy and enjoyable stay. Visit them for a stress-free vacation. You can view the Flamingo Motel at www.flamingomotel.com, or call 850-234-2232 to make reservations, request a brochure, or simply ask questions. Make the Flamingo Motel your choice for your next Panama City Beach getaway! You will not be sorry.

Liz *and* Jane

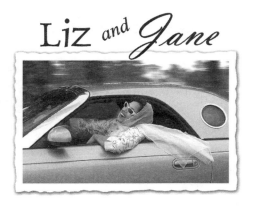

Their clothes are called "beachy keen," "artistically unique" and "comfortably fun." That could also describe them—designers Liz and Janie Bennett, friends, sisters-in-law and owners of one of Florida's most successful ladies clothing companies—Liz and Jane. These two Florida-born girls are themselves amazed at the incredible roller-coaster ride of success they have been on since starting their clothing line 11 years ago. Their husbands, brothers Mike and Neel, had a "beach business." They rented Wave Runners, parasails, and chairs. The girls decided to try their hand at making something "beachy" to sell, and began tie dying T-shirts in their carports. They sold their brightly colored T's and leggings to everyone they knew in Panama City and then took the plunge and headed to the Atlanta Apparel Mart where they met their first sales rep. They can hardly remember the rest—it all started happening so fast. They went from making 3,000 pieces a year to delivering 30,000 items a month! You'll find their line in stores like Nordstrom's and high-end specialty stores all across the country, and right here at 15606 Front Beach Rd. in Panama City Beach. You may also visit the Silver Sands Factory Store Mall in Destin at 10746 Emerald Coast Pkwy. and the Company Store at The Summit in Birmingham, AL.

Liz and Jane clothes are fun, comfortable, and easy to "live in." The designs are colorful and artistic. Women love the easy fit of the separates whether they are a fitted style or a fuller cut for the fuller figure. They are just fun to wear! Liz and Jane in Panama City Beach is open Monday-Saturday 9 am-6 pm and Sunday 10 am-5 pm. Visit www.lizandjane.com or call 850-234-7522 for more information.

Restaurants & Seafood Markets

Two large fireplaces book-end the grand dining area, creating a warm, relaxing atmosphere at the Boar's Head Restaurant & Tavern. The Ross family construct-ed the building at 17290 Front Beach Rd. in Panama City Beach in 1978, and family members have operated the Boar's Head Restaurant & Tavern ever since. They offer award-winning prime rib, wild game, and choice aged steaks, as well as red snap-per, grouper, tuna, shrimp, and oysters in delicious recipes devel-oped over the last 25 years. The extensive menu also features suc-culent lobster dishes, including their specialty—Fried Lobster. Whether you like your meat or fish grilled; fried; stuffed; roasted; or blackened; there is truly something for everyone here! The Boar's Head Restaurant & Tavern has garnered the award for "Bay County's Best Service," "Bay County's Best Special Occasion Restaurant," and "Bay County's Best Prime Rib." The extensive wine selection has been recognized by *Wine Spectator Magazine* and the restaurant has been recommended by *Florida Trend Magazine*, Mobil and AAA. In-season the restaurant is open daily for dinner at 4:30 pm. For off-season hours, call 850-234-6628 or visit www.boarsheadrestaurant.com.

Capt. Anderson's

R E S T A U R A N T
& W A T E R F R O N T M A R K E T

When we say Capt. Anderson's is an award-winning restaurant, we're not kidding. Here are just a few of its accolades: •Given *Southern Living Magazine's* Reader's Choice Award eight years for the best seafood restaurant in the South Eastern United States •Given *Wine Spectator Magazine's* Award of Excellence four years •Honored with *Florida Trend Magazine's* Golden Spoon Award 15 years. A Panama City Beach landmark at 5551 N. Lagoon Dr., Capt. Anderson's has been satisfying locals and visitors with its consistently delicious seafood and steaks, signature breads, and fresh baked desserts for more than 36 years. It is located dockside at Grand Lagoon, with a panoramic view of the fishing and sight-seeing boats, so dine early and watch the fleet unload. The atmosphere is casual, relaxed, and friendly. The extensive menu includes charcoal broiled Red Snapper, Grouper, and Steaks; Fried Crab Fingers; Grilled Bay Shrimp; Crab Meat au Gratin; and Florida Lobster Thermidor. You'll also find a variety of oils, olives, cheeses, pastries, and Greek specialty foods in the Waterfront Market.

Owners Jimmy and Johnny Patronis have owned the restaurant since 1967, but gratefully acknowledge Captains Walt and Max Anderson's unique contribution to local history with the opening of Capt. Anderson's in 1958. Many of the employees have been with the restaurant since the beginning, and this feeling extends to every customer. The restaurant and market open daily (except Sunday) at 4 pm. Call 850-234-2225 for more information, or visit www.captanderson.com online. Oh, and don't miss out on the fifth edition of "The Captain's Classics Cookbook." It will make a wonderful souvenir!

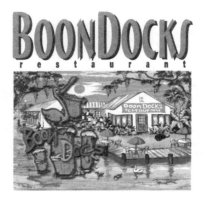

It could possibly be described as being "out in the Boondocks," and that's exactly what Hilary Head named this wonderful family seafood restaurant overlooking the Intracoastal Waterway. Boon Docks has the ambience of a friendly country bay home. Be sure to start your meal with the famous "fried pickles," battered and fried to a golden brown, and served with homemade Ranch dressing. Leave off the old tires and seaweed, and you'll have Hilary's signature dish—Boat Trash, a combination of shrimp, oysters, grouper, and deviled crab. If you are not a seafood lover, you will love the grilled rib eye steaks or spicy chicken breasts. Mama and Grandma make the desserts, so be sure to save room for these delicious homemade treats.

Boon Docks Restaurant is located at 14854 Bay View Cir. in Panama City Beach, a little hard to find, but well worth the search. From Hwy. 98 turn on Hwy. 79, go four miles, turn right on School Rd. to a four-way stop, turn left and go down to the bay. Boon Docks will be on your right. Open year round. Please call 850-230-0005 for seasonal hours.

MORE–NOT FISHY COOKING TIPS

Boil any fish bones, skin, or parts after cleaning. This makes a great stock for later.

—Peggy Adams

Essentials Salon & Boutique

Nan Lueck and Lisa Sutton have been partners and doing hair, nails and more for more than 20 years. If you like to be pampered, (frankly who doesn't?) Essentials Salon & Boutique is a must visit. You'll feel at home in this full-service salon. You can have your hair fixed, your nails done, receive a massage, or experience all three! Essentials has a home atmosphere, which is very welcoming and you'll always find fresh ground coffee, sodas, water, and snacks available. Nan and Lisa also have gifts within their shop, which include all sorts of knick-knacks, candles, flowers, and more. Essentials Salon & Boutique is located at 12119 Panama City Beach Pkwy., in the Lyndell Centre, a new shopping complex in Panama City Beach. There are no set hours, so you need to call ahead for an appointment. Essentials is open Monday-Saturday, but closed on Sunday. Call 850-236-5664. And, when you find yourself in the Panama City Beach area, give Nan and Lisa a call and indulge yourself in the better things of life.

DISCOVER
PENSACOLA / PENSACOLA BEACH
PACE / GULF BREEZE

PENSACOLA

Yesterday and Today

Originally settled in 1559 by Spanish explorer Don Tristan de Luna, and permanently settled in 1698, Pensacola is Florida's oldest European settlement. It has been described as, "where the New World began." Even in those long-ago days, this northern shore of the Gulf of Mexico was an ancient explorer's dream. Stories tell of de Luna's crew members leaping, horses and all, into the surf for days of water fun. Flags of five nations have flown over the city in the past four centuries, and it remains to this day a city very influenced by its multi-cultural history. This vibrant area on Florida's Emerald Coast is recognized for its international businesses, manufacturing, and, of course, the Pensacola Naval Air Station.

Pensacola has been nicknamed the "Cradle of Naval Aviation." From the original Spanish forts to the Nimitz class carrier, military experts have counted on the natural harbor and geographical importance of Pensacola to defend the United States. In fact, it was chosen as the sight of the first naval aeronautical installation in 1914 because of its location on the Gulf of Mexico. One of the most famous organizations to originate in Pensacola was, of course, the Blue Angels. Since 1946 they have thrilled millions of visitors all over the world, and have been instrumental in recruiting many men and women to the Navy. If you are visiting during November, you'll be able to see their final performance of the year from Sherman Field. However, no matter when you are in Pensacola, make sure to visit the Naval Museum. We did and we were very impressed.

Today's Pensacola is a diverse community, and a contradiction in character. It has all of the big beach city excitement and amenities, yet retains its small-town Southern charm. Life here is sophisticated and cosmopolitan, yet casual and charming. We know you will agree that it's a perfect place to play!

PENSACOLA BEACH

Fun In the Sun

You can't miss it! A giant neon sign with a colorful billfish over it says, "Turn right—Pensacola Beach, Scenic Drive along Gulf of Mexico." Only 75 years ago, this "scenic drive" would only have included the sunrises, sunsets, and dancing dolphins. The view began to change drastically in 1931, when the Pensacola Bay Bridge across the Santa Rosa Sound was built, ushering in new businesses, first time visitors, and a whole new life for this beautiful beach. Today, only about 3,000 residents call Pensacola Beach home, but more than 3 million cars cross the bridge annually for fun, sun, and great family memories. It is a favorite destination for family vacations, spring breaks, or gal pal "road trips." Pensacola Beach was featured on the Travel Channel's "Top Secret Beaches of the World" series in 2002. The rich Spanish and French histories of Pensacola have culminated in many "Fiesta" and "Mardi Gras" events that draw visitors from across the state. And, to make these easy events to enjoy, you'll find free trolleys running up and down the beach. The red sunsets, white beaches, and Navy Blue Angels are hard to beat. The powder white sand is made from quartz, which washes down from the Appalachian Mountains. It is so fine; it makes a "barking" sound as it squishes between your toes. There is so much for you and your family to do together, so plan some time to explore the boating, sailing, fishing, and diving opportunities that abound. Ladies get their "Day Out" in the sun each year, in one of the city's most anticipated events. It is an "all girl regatta" where bikini-clad girls take to the sea in sailboats in a festive and fun competition. (This is one time your guys won't mind tagging along!)

PACE

Special Times, Family Fun

This energetic, fast-growing bay community was originally called Florida Town, established by William Barnett in 1821. It was the site of his lumber mill. The name Pace was not created until 1907 when James C. Pace opened the Pace Mill. The town sports a friendly, hometown atmosphere, where the crack of a bat hitting the softball and children laughing are soothing sounds of everyday, normal living.

GULF BREEZE

Then and Now

Located on a peninsula that stretches between the city of Pensacola and Santa Rosa Island, Gulf Breeze is just that—a delightful breath of fresh air; 300 days of sunshine each year; and, of course, access to the famous Gulf beaches. Gulf Breeze shares the rich history of Pensacola Bay, with its first inhabitants dating back a thousand years. Mounds of shells are a testament to the presence of the first Native Americans who feasted on the blessings from the sea. In 1931 a concrete drawbridge connected this strip of land to Pensacola, changing the life of Gulf Breeze forever. In 1936, Gulf Breeze Cottages and Store opened a post office branch where the Beach Road Plaza now stands, and the community had its name. When the bay bridge was improved in 1960, the community began to really expand and take on the life of a real town—one offering everything from unspoiled natural beauty and a laid-back lifestyle to a unique community of wonderful cultural and shopping opportunities. Local shops are an eclectic blend of art, antiques, clothing, and gift boutiques.

For more information on Pensacola, contact the Pensacola Chamber of Commerce at 800-608-3479 or 850-438-4081, or visit online at www.pensacolachamber.com.

For more information on Pensacola Beach, call the Pensacola Beach Chamber of Commerce at 800-635-4803 or 850-932-1500, or visit www.visitpensacolabeach.com online.

For more information on Pace, contact the Pace Chamber of Commerce at 850-994-9633, or visit www.pacechamber.com online.

For more information on Gulf Breeze, call the Gulf Breeze Chamber of Commerce at 850-932-7888, or visit www.gulfbreezechamber.com online.

Pensacola/Pensacola Beach Pace / Gulf Breeze Fairs Festivals & Fun

January
- Annual Polar Bear Dip
- Martin Luther King Jr. Parade
- Annual Antique Show & Sale

February
- Mardi Gras Street Party/Parades/Activities
- Blue Angel Marathon
- Cajun Fest
- Double Bridge Run
- Big Band Concert Series

March
- Gulf Breeze "Celebrates the Arts"
- Annual Kite Flying Contest
- Annual Santa Rosa Celebrates the Arts
- Gulf Coast Renaissance Festival
- Pace Patriot Festival
- Gallery Night
- Festival of Nations
- Pensacola Bay International Film & Television Festival

April
- Pace Festival Days
- Annual Easter Egg Hunt/Bonnet Contest
- Pensacola Jazz Fest

April cont.

Annual Pensacola Crawfish Festival
GraceFest
Santa Rosa County Fair
Festival on the Green
Sunny Beaches Rod Run
British Car Show
Easter Sunrise Services by the Sea
The Blue Angel Classic (Senior PGA Tournament)
Annual Interstate Mullet Toss

May

Crawfish Creole Fiesta
Annual LobsterFest
Symphony by the Sea
Annual Firefighters' Competition
The Florida SpringFest
Annual Starlight Bike Ride
Scottish Festival

June

Fiesta Mass
Fiesta Parade of Champions
Fiesta of Five Flags De Luna Landing Fest
Bud Light King Mackerel/Cobia Tournament
DeLuna's Landing Ceremony
Sand Sculpting Contest
Elks Flag Day Ceremony

July

Red, White and Blues Week
Pensacola Beach Air Show
Fireworks
Pensacola International Billfish Tournament
Gallery Night

August

Bushwacker & Music Festival

September

SRI Triathlon
LobsterFest
Annual Cellular South Seafood Festival
Pensacola Seafood Festival
Annual Antique Auto Show
Santa Rosa County Fair

October
   Greek Festival
   The Zoo Boo
   Oktoberfest
   Jay Peanut Festival
   Haunted House Walking and Trolley Tours
   Annual Pet Fest
   Jingle Bell Jubilee

November
   Great Gulfcoast Arts Festival
   Blue Angels Homecoming Air Show
   Veterans' Day Parade
   Frank Brown Songwriter's Festival
   Zoo Lights
   Indian Days Celebration

December
   Gulf Breeze Annual Holiday Parade
   Lighted Boat Parade
   Pace Christmas Parade
   St. Anne's Christmas Lights
   Zoo Lights
   St. Christopher's Annual Christmas Caravan
   Christmas Parade
   Christmas Walk in Seville Square
   New Year's Eve Fireworks Celebration

Antiques

World-class antiques are not a world away—they are at Jackson Hill Antiques & Interiors, 823 E. Jackson St. in Pensacola. It is often described as the city's most beautiful shop. Located in Pensacola's East Hill Historic District, the 15 showrooms in two side-by-side historic homes are full of estate silver, china, crystal, jewelry and fine home accessories and furnishings. Items are displayed in room-style settings and decorating advice is readily given if requested. The warm, friendly atmosphere makes you feel right at home and complimentary refreshments are offered daily. Hours are Monday-Friday 10 am-5 pm and Saturday 10 am-4 pm. For more information, call 850-470-0668. *(Color picture featured in front section of the book.)*

Magnolia
ANTIQUE MALL

"A veritable emporium of curiosities and collectibles."

After spending years shopping flea markets, antique stores, and estate sales, and refinishing the treasures she found, Pamela Long knew that one day she wanted to have her own antique source. She built Magnolia Antique Mall at 4390 Gulf Breeze Pkwy. (Hwy. 98) in Gulf Breeze, and now says, "I am doing exactly what I love to do!" You will love visiting this beautiful, elegantly finished, 11,000-square-foot showroom filled with wonderful mahogany furniture, primitives, European antiques, and rare collectibles like Flow Blue Transferware. Whether you collect vintage clothing and acces-

sories; antique kitchen gadgets; estate silver and crystal; or antique toys and books; you'll find it here! Magnolia Antique Mall is open Monday-Saturday 10 am-5:30 pm and Sunday noon-5:30 pm. Call 850-932-2992.

 isteria Café

Karina (Karen) Cleveland-Morelli grew up cooking with her mother and grandmothers, learning the secrets that can only be discovered with time and love. It was her long-time dream to have a small, European-style cozy café where people could relax with friends over healthy gourmet food, enjoy conversation and wine, or visit over a delectable dessert and gourmet coffee. Wisteria Café, 221 E. Zarragossa St. in the heart of Historic Olde Seville Square in Pensacola, is that dream come true. The menu is varied with several specialty salads and sandwiches. Favorites of the downtown crowd are the Wisteria—Melt-in-your-mouth Roast Beef Sandwich, and the Apple Pie-Wisteria. Open 11 am-3 pm Sunday, Tuesday and Wednesday, and Thursday-Saturday 11 am-10 pm. Call 850-438-8188.

RESTAURANT

Russell Scarritt started as a busboy at Jamie's Restaurant in 1981 and today, he and his wife Linda, are the owners. Jamie's, at 424 E. Zarragossa St. in Pensacola, has been awarded *Florida Trend Magazine's* Golden Spoon Award along with *Wine Spectator Magazine's* Award of Excellence. The cuisine is French with a county flair. Be sure to try the award-winning crab cakes! And on weekend nights, stop by and listen to classical guitarist Paul Gerard. For more information, call 850-434-2911.

Norma Fleming Murray says in an excerpt from her best-selling cookbook "As Always: Recipes and Remembrances from Norma's" that the most important words her husband ever spoke to her were: "If this is what you want to do, I'll help you. It's your turn now." This was his reaction to her decision to open her own café. She now has three locations in Pensacola: Norma's Café in Dillards, Cordova Mall on 9th Ave.; Norma's On The Run at 28 N. Palafox St. in downtown Pensacola; and Norma's By The Bay at 500 Bayfront Pkwy. At each one, you'll be treated to delicious chick-

en salad, seafood gumbo, poppy seed bread, and more. The atmosphere is intimate and elegant, and the food is fresh and delicious! Café hours are 10:30 am-2:30 pm Monday-Friday at the downtown locations, and 11 am-3 pm Monday-Saturday at the mall. Call 850-434-8646 for cookbook information.

You will feel quite welcome at this award-winning eatery. Open Monday-Friday from 11 am-3 pm, chef Erika Thomas offers an upscale lunch menu in a casual elegant setting. Try one of the house specialties—wasabi crusted grouper or the famous stuffed portabello sandwich. Complimenting the menu selections is the atmosphere. The Portabello Market is located at 400 S. Jefferson St. inside the three-story brick atrium of the Pensacola Cultural Center.

The building is also the home of the Pensacola Little Theater and was the location of the county jail from 1912-1926. The Portabello Market also offers delivery, take-out, catered luncheons and dinners, as well as hosts open houses, cocktail parties and weddings. Call 850-439-6545 or visit www.agourmetoccasion.com online.

"If you've tasted better barbecue, we want to know about it," challenge the folks at Billy Bob's, but we can tell you right now—you won't! With a secret family recipe, Ben and Sherry Rogers serve up barbecue smoked over pecan wood for 14 hours. Their famous Carolina hand-pulled pork is so delicious, you'll want to eat it without sauce. Their sauces, however, are incredible. Choose from clear Carolina style vinegar, traditional mild or spicy, or mayonnaise and mustard based sauces. Whether you are having a backyard get together for a few, or a black tie affair for hundreds, Billy Bob's can cater five to 500 pounds of meat and side dishes ready to eat or chilled for travel. You'll love the meat; succulent spare ribs; tender chicken; spicy sausage; delectable turkey; and thick-sliced brisket. Visit Billy Bob's at 911 Gulf Breeze Pkwy. in Gulf Breeze, daily 11 am-9 pm. Visit www.billybobsbarbecue.com or call 850-934-2999.

THE FISH HOUSE & ATLAS OYSTER HOUSE

For waterfront dining, stop by The Fish House, 600 Barracks St. in Pensacola, where the locals go for delicious Southern-style seafood, fresh-off-the-dock specials, and sushi. Enjoy a full-service bar and choose from more than 300 hand-picked varieties of wine. Atlas Oyster House serves the finest oysters available seasonally, a full seafood menu, and the same Grits à Ya Ya that Chef Jim Shirley made famous at The Fish House next door. Opens daily at 11 am. Call 850-470-0003 or visit www.goodgrits.com.

Jackson's

"Southern charm, Superb Steaks and Seafood" describes this award-winning restaurant at 400 S. Palafox St. in Pensacola. Jackson's has been voted one of Florida's Top 25 Restaurants, and received the "Golden Spoon Award" in 2002 and 2003. Open daily for dinner and happy hour at 5:30 pm. Call 850-469-9898 or visit online at www.jacksonsrestaurant.com.

THE CRAB TRAP

Be sure and check out The Crab Trap in Pensacola, 16495 Perdido Key Dr., 850-492-8888. See page 45 for full details.

Enter this fresh food market and you are immediately surrounded by the sights, sounds, and smells of a busy kitchen at work. The entire kitchen is open, and you'll see the staff preparing more than 60 entrees; salads; wraps; breads; desserts; and various side dishes. The food is prepared daily and then displayed on colorful platters inside large refrigerated display cases. The friendly, helpful staff will greet you and help you select your favorite items, and either package them for travel or prepare them to eat on the beautifully landscaped garden patio. Not sure of a selection? You'll be encouraged to sample anything in the cases. The food at Simply Delicious, 1217 N. 9th Ave. in Pensacola, offers the kinds of dishes you would expect in New York or San Francisco. Executive chef Ellen Deaver uses her classical training and passion for food to create entrees with flavors and taste combinations from all over the world. Simply Delicious is open Monday-Saturday from 10 am-7 pm. Having a special event? Plan ahead and Ellen will create a special menu just for you. Call 850-439-2800. Don't miss this unique and wonderful market. It's a true "find," and has become a "must see" destination on the Gulf Coast.

APPETITE for life

The mission of Appetite for Life, 1842 W. Cervantes St., is to prepare and deliver freshly-cooked meals to persons living with HIV/AIDS and other documented terminal illnesses in the Pensacola area. This caring bunch has been doing just that since June 1997, when the first meals were delivered.

Through grants, private donations, and the work of volunteers, more than 175,000 meals had been served as of November 2002. In order to help fund this work, Appetite for Life began offering a catering service in 1999. Today, this growing business caters events such as wedding receptions; birthdays; Bar Mitzvahs; private parties; civic group functions and church happenings in the Pensacola area. Hours are Monday-Friday 9 am-5 pm and Saturday 9 am-2 pm. Call 850-470-9111 or www.appetite4life.org online.

PENSACOLA - THE GRAND

Standing majestically against the backdrop of the beautiful blue Florida sky, at 200 E. Gregory St., the Crowne Plaza Pensacola Grand Hotel brings vibrant life and historical charm to the downtown area. Its 150-foot tower is by far the tallest building in the Pensacola area, and the remodeled historic L & N train depot now serves as the hotel's entrance lobby, lounges, meeting rooms, and administration offices. Built in 1912, the depot is listed as an important landmark. A unique rectangular bar with a large screen television is found inside the "CAVU" club, and the

"1912" Restaurant features Old World charm. Lavish custom-made furnishings are employed in the 212 decorated guest rooms, and guests have access to a beautiful heated swimming pool, fitness center, business center, and in-room dining options. For more information, call 850-433-3336, 800-348-3336 or visit online at www.pensacolagrandhotel.com.

Resting on the shore of Pensacola Bay, the Bay Beach Inn, 51 Gulf Breeze Pkwy. in Gulf Breeze welcomes its visitors with balmy breezes and the refreshing aroma of the bay. Each guest room is equipped with such perks as cable television, data ports, coffee makers, and hair dryers. You'll also enjoy the Inn's acclaimed restaurant—Bon Appetit. This waterfront café offers a view almost as breathtaking as its delectable dishes. The café offers complimentary beer and wine as well as spectacular sunsets and special occasion catering. Don't miss the Sunday champagne brunch overlooking the bay. Call the café at 850-932-3967 or visit daily 7 am to 2 pm and 5 to 9 pm. The Inn is open 24-hours daily. For more information, call 850-932-2214 or visit www.baybeachinn.com.

PENSACOLA BEACH PROPERTIES

If you are looking for a place to stay in Northwest Florida, then let Pensacola Beach Properties Inc. find it for you. This family-owned-and-operated business goes the extra mile to help you locate the best vacation rentals and real estate sales on Pensacola Beach. Real Estate Broker/Owner Beth Schachner and rental manager Traci Land are sisters. They manage one to five bedroom condos, townhouses, and houses on fabulous Pensacola Beach. An example of what they have to offer is located on Calle Bonita—this is a Gulf front, five bedroom, four-and-a-half bath, deluxe townhouse. Another example is found at Starboard Village, which is a three bedroom, three bath, Gulf front townhouse with a pool at the complex. These are just two of the many properties the sisters have available. Hours are Monday-Friday 8 am-5 pm and Saturday 9 am-5 pm, so stop by! Located at 50 Fort Pickens Road. Call 800-497-7321, 850-934-0099 or visit www.pensacolabeachproperty.com.

The Linen Corner

This charming little house at 698 W. Garden St. in Pensacola is the perfect setting for all of the wonderful fashion accessories and special gifts you'll find inside The Linen Corner. Owners Robin Ellinor and Cheryl Hart and clothing buyer Shelia Hogue are as special as their store, and they love providing their customers with special personal attention.

Each of the rooms in the home is decorated with beautiful things—ladies clothing; jewelry; fashion accessories; and special gift items that will delight anyone on your list. The Linen Corner has been a local favorite for more than 30 years for several reasons:

everyone loves the girls who work at The Linen Corner; they feel welcomed each time they visit; and know that they will consistently find unique items as well as beautiful clothing with the perfect accessories. Open Monday-Friday 10 am-5 pm and Saturday until 4 pm. Call 850-438-9887.

The Market

Anne Frechette and her mother Tish Childs, owners of The Market, and Peggy Woolverton, owner of Mainly Shoes, share the same shop at 248 W. Garden St. in Pensacola. The Market offers everything from jeans to eveningwear. Mainly Shoes carries both traditional and trendy shoe lines—great blends of cutting-edge designers, as well as shoes for those seeking comfort with style. Open Monday-Friday 10 am-5 pm and Saturday 'til 4 pm. Call 850-434-3012 or 850-438-7114.

mainly shoes

Madame De Elegance

Madame De Elegance takes ladies back to a time when women experienced class and elegance while shopping— they deliver the finest in ladies' ready-to-wear with "champagne service." The store was inspired by the trade of a precious diamond ring for a unique, one-of-a-kind antique gown in 1983 by owner Helan White. You'll find stylish casual outfits to gala gowns and luxurious custom-tailored furs. Visit Tuesday-Friday 10 am-5 pm, Saturday 10 am-4 pm and Monday by appointment. Madame De Elegance is located at 1116 N. 9th Ave. in Pensacola. Call 850-438-0012 or visit www.mdelegance.com. *(Color picture featured in front section of the book.)*

...where fashion and beauty blend together with plenty of sass. This is a one-stop shop for women who crave the best selections of clothing and accessories, as well as beauty and bath care. Curve For Body & Soul is located at 280 N. Palafox St. in Pensacola's historical downtown. Built in the early 1940s, the building sports a large storefront window that is always filled with enticing clothing, jewelry, accessories, and fun items for your "body & soul." *The Independent Florida Sun* named Curve the "2003 First Place Winner for Best Women's Boutique and Best Casual/Hip Clothing." You'll find contemporary and staple pieces of clothing for the very fashion-minded, as well as bridesmaid dresses from Nicole Miller and BCBG to compliment your perfect day. Their upscale bath and beauty products will make you look and feel beautiful. Stop by Monday-Friday 10 am-5 pm and Saturday 11 am-4 pm. Call 850-430-4333.

You will feel welcome when you stop by and visit Connie Taylor. For more than eight years Connie has been providing her clientele with the latest in home décor. Taylor's Gifts and Home Décor, 4450 Woodbine Rd. in Pace, is a cozy little cottage full of home accessories and a gift line for all occasions. You'll find Vera Bradley handbags and travel accessories; Lampe Berger (which is an air cleansing system from France); framed art; lamps; windchimes and more! We loved the silver crosses in all shapes and sizes. There is so much to see, and soon there will be more. Connie has plans to expand to a larger location in the future. Be sure to stop in and get some beautiful ideas for decorating your home. The store is open Monday-Saturday from 9:30 am-5 pm. Call 850-995-4682.

As the name suggests, Eclectic Home: A Marketplace, offers a unique variety of treasures. Co-owners Angie Denmon and Kelley Amos have brought together a small group of retailers who share the "marketplace" to showcase everything from antique and new home furnishings to room sprays and lotions. The store is nestled in the historic Brent Building at 19 S. Palafox Place in Pensacola, and is open Tuesday-Friday 10 am-6 pm, and Saturday 10 am-4 pm. Call 850-435-9500.

McAlpin Interiors

The beautifully restored home at 900 E. Moreno St. (corner of Ninth Ave.) in Pensacola was built during the 1890s as a dairy farm, but today the handsomely decorated rooms hold exquisite antiques and treasures. McAlpin Interiors will inspire you to create beauty in your own home. You'll find English, French, and Continental antique furniture and silver serving pieces, custom-made lamps and lampshades, framed art, and handmade rugs.

Owner Clifford Stiles "Tip" McAlpin, has a B. A. from the University of Alabama, and studied at the Parson's School of Design in Paris. He is a member of ASID and holds a state license as an interior designer in Florida. You will appreciate his professional, yet personal help in selecting the perfect piece for your home. McAlpin Interiors has one of the city's favorite bridal registries. Store hours are Monday-Friday 9:30 am-5 pm and Saturday until 4 pm. Call 850-438-8345.

THE PILLARS
Ron White Interiors

The Pillars, 12 S. Palafox Pl. in Pensacola, offers a wide variety of home furnishings, accessories, lighting, and gifts, as well as custom draperies and bedspreads. Decorator Ron White's work has been featured in *Southern Living* and *Women's World* magazines. Visit his store Monday-Friday 10 am-5 pm or Saturday until 3 pm. Call 850-470-2627 for more information.

IMPORTERS SINCE 1967

Since 1967, Artesana has been an importer of wonderful things for Pensacola's most discerning shoppers. Artesana specializes in wooden plates, cookware, lamps, linens, Vietri, enamelware, Crabtree & Evelyn, baby and wedding gifts, and custom-printed and engraved invitations. Artesana is the largest importer of wooden dinnerware in the Southeast. Located at 242 W. Garden St.; stop by Monday-Saturday 10 am-5 pm. Call 850-433-4001 or visit www.artesanagifts.com online.

The playful, creative name is just the first intriguing attribute of this unique and charming garden and home boutique at 501 N. 9th Ave. This store features gorgeous gifts and home décor, as well as a mecca of Italian terra-cotta pots and garden accessories. Co-owner Quinn Stinson says he "grew up in flea markets," while co-owner Jim Rigsbee, on the other hand, "in a family of gallery owners and auctioneers." When these two gifted men combined their talents and ideas, the result was . . . duh. . . .a fabulous garden and home shop that is "everyone's favorite place to shop." In fact, "duh" was voted #1 Gift Shop in Pensacola. Check out duh's feature in the November 2003 *Southern Living*! The shop is open Monday-Saturday 9 am-6 pm and Sunday 1-5 pm. Call 850-439-0640.

Jewelry

Trinity Collection

Owners Jodi Allen and Ione Calhoon pride themselves on having unique items not found in other jewelry stores. Trinity Collection is well-known for its exquisite sterling and 14K gold crosses and religious jewelry handmade in their studio. Trinity Collection also offers a variety of unusual precious and semi-precious gemstone jewelry. If it is not a piece made in their studio, it is carefully selected by the owners for beauty of design, individual quality, craftsmanship and value.

Mark your life's most important celebrations with a unique and meaningful gift from Trinity Collection. Stop by downtown, at 422 N. Palafox in Pensacola, between Garden and Cervantes...on the hill. Hours are Tuesday-Saturday 10 am-5 pm. Call 800-442-0030 or 850-433-0005 or visit www.trinitycollection.com online.

Salons, Spas & Indulgence

The owners call it "European Spa Treatments in a Steel Magnolias atmosphere!" Radiante Jacqueline Day Spa at 1521 N. Ninth Ave. in Pensacola prides itself on the quality of the European spa and full-service salon services. Owner Jacqueline Cummins has been trained in Europe in order to offer her patrons the cutting edge in "beauty by health," such as Hydrotherapy, Balneotherapy, Aromatherapy, and Thalossotherapy. Beauty services include hair styling; manicure and pedicure; full body waxing; facials; body treatments; airbrush tanning; massage; and expert make up application. For your sheer well-being, Darphin Skin Care products, which combine the therapeutic and soothing qualities of Aromatherapy, essential vitamins, and active molecules derived from plants, are available.

For information, call 850-432-0939. Ask about seasonal specials. The spa is open Monday-Saturday, 9 am–6 pm.

This beautiful and sophisticated salon "studio" has been a dream come true for owners Rodney Kehl and Pat Jolly, who decided to make Pensacola their home after visiting from Atlanta. Their vision was to offer clients a beautiful experience, a relaxing environment, and experts who truly enjoyed helping others. Mission accomplished! Studio Twenty-8 is located in the historical area of old Pensacola at 28 S. Palafox Place in a building with an Old New Orleans design. Rodney, Jolly and their staff offer a full line of services including color specialist, all nail services, massage therapy, advanced skin care, and the relaxing and effective facial peel called microdermabrasion. Something for everyone— Ladies and Gents! Studio Twenty-8 is open Tuesday-Friday 9 am-5 pm and Saturday 8 am-4 pm. Call 850-438-2028 or visit www.studiotwenty-8.com online.

Some people are alive only because it's illegal to kill them.
—Unknown

 **JOE PATTI**
SEAFOOD COMPANY, INC.

Although Joe and Anna Patti were born less than 10 miles apart in their native Sicily, they did not meet each other until 1928, after both had immigrated to Pensacola. Captain Joe caught fresh bay shrimp, and Anna sold them from the back porch of their modest dwelling. Although these family founders are no longer here, the Patti family (Frank and Maria) continues to make Joe Patti Seafood Co. a huge success. Since its beginnings in 1935, it has become world renowned for its fresh and frozen seafood. It's easy to find the store; look for the fishing boats on the bay behind the market at the foot of "A" Street and Main. You'll love the seafood and service. Joe Patti's Seafood Co. is open daily 7 am-7 pm. Visit www.joepattis.com online or call 850-432-3315.

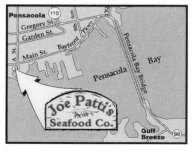

Specialty Shops

 New World Rugs

 Ginger Weible prides herself on not only selling the best hand-knotted rugs, but also finding "good homes for them." At Ginger's stores, Oasis/New World Rugs, you can tell she travels extensively to find uniquely beautiful rugs for her stores. You will find rugs by Tufenkian, Megerian, and Samad in Ginger's stores, and many one-of-a-kind carpets from smaller weavers. Stop by both locations—in Pensacola at 104 S. Palafox St. and in Destin at 2441 Hwy. 98 W. At Oasis you will see rugs from Pakistan, India, China, Persia, Egypt, and even Romania. Every rug is beautiful in Ginger's stores because each one is hand- picked.

Open Monday-Friday 10 am-4:30 pm and by appointment only on Saturday and Sunday, visit www.oasisrugs.com or call 850-470-9600 for Pensacola, or 850-622-9722 for the Destin area store located in Santa Rosa Beach.

When it comes to home décor shops, variety is one of the first things a customer should look for—and that is one thing that Galleria Lamps and Shades has plenty of! Located at 2435 N. 12th Ave. in Pensacola, this shop's range from lamps to antiques and one-of-a-kind home stylings will make you glad you stopped in. Galleria Lamps and Shades also offers a repair service to help keep your beautiful purchases looking new. Open Monday-Saturday 9 am-5pm. Call 850-432-3335.

Christine Baehr actually started her business from her home at the early age of 16! Today, her remarkable store at 5043 Bayou Blvd., A-2 in Pensacola is filled with beautiful displays of imprintable papers for all occasions. She offers customized invitations and specialty printing. Hours are Tuesday-Friday 10 am-4:30 pm and Saturday 10 am-2 pm. Call 850-476-7176.

DISCOVER SANTA ROSA BEACH

The beautiful beaches of South Walton County encompass 13 eclectic beach communities each with a personality all its own and more than 200 miles of tall, powder-white dunes, marshlands, fresh water springs, pine forests, bays, bayous and—of course—the famous crystalline waters of the Gulf of Mexico. There are a multitude of family-fun options to enjoy while visiting the area. Santa Rosa Beach is a great place to start.

The brilliant slice of paradise called Santa Rosa Beach is one of the oldest beach towns along Hwy. 30A. Named for the Santa Rosa Plantation, which was once a center for turpentine production, Santa Rosa Beach is the largest tract of land of all the South Walton beaches. Its famous attractions include Point Washington and Eden State Gardens and the beautiful Topsail Hill State Reserve—one of the state's most beautiful stretches of coastal property. Its beach, dunes, lake and swamp areas remain relatively untouched since the first European adventurers landed almost 500 years ago.

Tee Time

Golfers praise their experiences at the Santa Rosa Golf and Beach Club, and *Golf Magazine* calls it "the purest golf in the Florida panhandle." Located between the beautiful beaches and the verdant woodlands, the incredible Santa Rosa Golf and Beach Club has been an integral part of the area's growth. Eighteen holes of challenging golf meander through powder white sands, glistening ponds and lush vegetation. Golfers will think they've died and gone to golf heaven!

Shop Till You Drop!

Free-spirited, "artsy," one-of-a-kind, and eclectic are all words to describe the shopping as well as the people in Santa Rosa Beach. Wandering roads lead to great shops and fascinating people tucked in the corners of this area. A truly unique shopping experience is waiting. Enjoy your "Day Out!"

For more information on Santa Rosa Beach, call Beaches of South Walton Tourist Development Council at 800-822-6877 or 850-267-1216 or visit www.beachesofsouthwalton.com online.

Santa Rosa Beach
Fairs Festivals & Fun

October
Flutterby Festival

December
Candlelight Tour at Eden

Attractions, Entertainment, Special Events & Weddings

WEDDING & EVENT PLANNING

Imagine standing under an arbor of beautiful flowers on beautiful white sand at sunset, saying "I do" to the love of your life. Whether you envision a private wedding on the beach or a tropical extravaganza, Jennifer Warwick and JoAnne Stapleton will make your wedding dreams come true. This talented mother-daughter team are the creative force behind the wedding and event planning business, "It's A Shore Thing," located in Santa Rosa Beach. Their specialty—you guessed it—perfect weddings and special events "on or near the beach!" A wedding they coordinated at WaterColor Resort was featured in the Summer 2003 issue of Southern Living Weddings. Leave everything to Jennifer and JoAnne. It's a "Shore Thing" that your wedding will be the most romantic memory of your life. For information visit online at www.itsashorething.net or call 850-259-3090 or, 850-259-3088.

Wetland Wilderness Adventures, Inc.

For an unforgettable adventure in "Old Florida," schedule a leisurely tour down the Choctawatchee River aboard Captain Kent Mundy's boat, *The Riverwatch*. Kids love cruising through the winding beds of sawgrass, thick swamps, and narrow passages of the river as Cap'n Mundy shares stories of his youth spent on the waters. *The Riverwatch* can take up to six people per trip for two- or four-hour tours. Call ahead for reservations at 850-534-0107 or visit www.southwaltonrivertours.com online.

The secret of staying young is to live honestly, eat slowly and lie about your age.

–Lucille Ball

Santa Rosa Golf & Beach Club

Delicious fare prepared by an award winning chef, romantic music, brilliant sunsets, and cocktails on the deck overlooking the beautiful Gulf of Mexico. If this sounds absolutely fabulous, then Santa Rosa Golf and Beach Club, Inc. at 4801 W. County Hwy. 30A in Santa Rosa Beach, is a must-stop for you. Although the club is member-owned, the public is always welcome to enjoy the restaurant's classy, yet casual atmosphere and deliciously creative food. Everything is incredible, from the fresh seafood appetizers and sig-

nature entrees to the decadent desserts. Live entertainment and dinner dancing are offered every Saturday evening, and the full bar allows you to enjoy your favorite libations while watching the dolphins wave goodnight. Santa Rosa Golf and Beach Club is open for lunch Tuesday-Friday 11:30 am-2:30 pm and for dinner Tuesday-Saturday 5-9 pm. Visit www.santarosaclub.com or call 850-267-1240.

Café Provence is Chef Michel's boyhood dream come true! With the help of a kitchen full of French cooks, he offers fine French cuisine such as: tableside crepes, chateaubriand and bread, and pastries made daily. Café Provence, 35 Musset Bayou Rd. in Santa Rosa Beach, opens for lunch Tuesday-Saturday 11 am-2 pm, for dinner Monday-Saturday 5:30 pm and Sunday brunch from 10 am-2 pm. Visit www.cafeprovenceusa.com online or call 850-622-3022. *(Color picture featured in front section of the book.)*

Don Pedro Alvarez came to America in 1971, leaving his family, but embracing the beginning of his future. He learned the restaurant business from the kitchen sink up before bringing his wife and children to help start his own restaurant, Don Pedro's Café & Bakery, 4942 Hwy. 98 in Santa Rosa Beach. We loved the fresh salsa and homemade tortilla chips. In fact, everything is homemade! Don Pedro's hours are Monday-Saturday 7 am-9 pm and Sunday until 2 pm. Call 850-267-0009.

This upbeat, very cool, beachside café is a Santa Rosa Beach favorite. George Barnes, a New Orleans native who vacationed on the Panhandle as a child, is as passionate about cooking as he is of taking care of his customers—his life on the beach as a restaurateur is a dream come true! George's signature salads, fresh seafood and New Orleans style dishes are all prepared with a coastal twist. Smiling Fish Café, on the corner of Hwy. 30A and Hwy. 393, is open daily for lunch and dinner. Call 850-622-3071.

A HIGHLAND HOUSE BED & BREAKFAST

Whether it's a leisurely get-away or an uninterrupted business meeting location you're searching for, A Highland's House, 4193 W. Scenic Hwy. 30A in Santa Rosa Beach, has what you need. With eight rooms, offering such amenities as a gulf view or a whirlpool for two, this bed and breakfast has it all.

Take advantage of the friendly conversation and gourmet food each morning in the dining room, too. In the words of owner Joan Robins and assistant Saronda Lewis, "We await your arrival!" Hours are 8 am-9 pm. For more information about the only beach-front B & B in the area, visit www.ahighlandshousebbinn.com or call 850-267-0110.

Relax in comfy Victorian style sofas and chairs; sip on a cup of gourmet coffee; indulge in a gooey cinnamon roll served on antique china; but please . . . gossip responsibly! The delightful owners of Miss Lucille's Gossip Parlor, Gulf Place in Santa Rosa Beach, have combined delicious treats with a relaxing atmosphere just for you! The menu offers espresso, decadent desserts, shaved ices, baked goods and sandwiches. And, a full ice cream parlor provides old-fashioned treats for all ages! Enjoy games, magazines, and free Internet access. The Parlor is open during the winter months daily 7:30 am-5 pm, and during the spring and summer until 9 pm. Call 850-267-BLAB.

For The Health Of It

What started as a small, health food store and one-room massage clinic has blossomed into Santa Rosa Beach's largest and finest natural food and massage therapy establishments. Choose from organic foods, fresh produce, vitamins and supplements or enjoy a smoothie or juice in the drink bar. The massage clinic features seven massage therapists. Visit at 2217 W. Hwy. 30A, Monday-Saturday 9:30 am-5:30 pm. Call 850-267-0558 or visit www.shopforthehealthofit.com.

Fashion, Accessories, Gifts & Home Décor

Located in the Shops at Gulf Place on Scenic Hwy. 30A in Santa Rosa Beach, Jewel Toffier offers women's clothing, accessories, jewelry and more, in a comfortable, cozy atmosphere.

Sisters Jodie and Kathy Stroble opened the shop in 2002 to fill a void in the clothing market for baby-boomer women and their lifestyles. Today, these fashion-wise women and their lively, dynamic staff create sensible wardrobes for women that span generations. You'll love Jewel T's, the Stroble sisters' own line of cotton T-shirts. Dress up more—slip into dresses and separates or, mix and match items for any occasion. Enjoy refreshments served daily, and stay awhile. Experience the art of wardrobing—assembling clothing that looks great, travels well, and wears well.

Open Monday-Saturday from 10 am-8 pm in season and until 6 pm off-season. For information, call 850-622-2358.

Beth Dillard's passion for interior design is evident as you walk into her home store/design studio. Her style draws from ethnic, as well as European design. Natural furnishings, fabrics, accessories, and artwork can be found here.

Beth Dillard's design work has been featured in *Coastal Living*, but you can see it at Notre Maison—Beth Dillard Interiors, County Rd. 30A in Gulf Place, Santa Rosa Beach. Call 850-622-2331.

Jewelry

Kent Ltd.

Angelia and Jim Waller love to tell the history of their beautiful jewelry and antique store—Kent, Ltd. Angelia says it all began when her mom, Linda, started buying antiques and estate items back in 1978. She had so much fun that her dad, Terry Kent Johnson, was soon "hooked," and they opened their first store in Pelham, Ga. Several more stores followed over the years in North Carolina and later in Florida. And, now, Angelia and Jim own their own store at 32 E. Hwy. 30A in Santa Rosa Beach. It is a beautiful store with wonderful lighting and creative displays. You'll find fabulous antique items, including: jewelry, fine linens, crystal, and more! The Wallers have a real talent for finding priceless pieces to collectible oddities. The store is great fun to explore, and the Wallers are extremely friendly and knowledgeable owners. Kent Ltd.—named after Angelia's dad—is open Monday-Saturday 10 am-6 pm. Call 850-231-6806.

ARRIAGA ORIGINALS

The beautifully handcrafted jewelry created at Arriaga Originals will hold you captive. Richard Arriaga specializes in sculpting wax molds, which are then cast with silver, gold, or both to create his very own original designs. He is also a master goldsmith and silversmith, creating one-of-a-kind pieces that are truly works of art. Customers may choose from precious or semi-precious stones, or unconventional materials like fossils or seashells for their designs. The shop at 39 Blue Gulf Dr. in Santa Rosa Beach is open Monday-Friday 10 am-6 pm and Saturday 11 am-5 pm. Call 850-622-5653.

*Out of my mind,
back in five minutes.*

—Unknown

Photography

THE ARD GALLERY

The Ard Gallery has captured the attention and rave reviews from both clients and artists from across the South, making this cleverly-named gallery a first choice for family and special occasion portraits.

Born and raised on Florida's Gulf Coast in Port St. Joe, Tim Ard was born into a very talented family. His parents owned and operated a florist and gift shop that still bears the family name. He was an instrumental part of the family operation and took control of the business in 1985 after the death of his mother. It was through the encouragement of his sister Jacque that Tim began his training in photography. He knew at once that this work would be the love of his professional life. With his natural creative flair and tremendous love for the business, Tim has built a reputation for excellence. His specialties include wedding, beach, and children's photography. As the father of two precious daughters, Ashton and Abby, Tim has a keen sense of how to relate to children, and is able to capture their wonderful, fleeting sense of wonder and whimsy. He says, "I love what I do . . . I do not go to work everyday, I go to play. The kids keep me young and humble, and it is an honor to record a family's memories in the art of photography . . . I am truly blessed!"

You will feel truly blessed to have a portrait by Tim Ard, and you will love visiting his gallery at 93 Madison St. in Freeport. Tim has also added a unique gift and accessories line to his business. You'll find Lux Candles, fine linens, exquisite home décor, and gifts for every occasion. Hours are Monday-Friday 9 am-5 pm. For more information, call 850-835-1911 or visit www.ardgallery.com.

Look for the landmark red building halfway between Destin and Panama City Beach, and you'll find a unique, multi-service dry cleaning business, and two very nice people. Ann and J. B. Kiefer re-located to Destin from New Orleans, and instantly connected with this emerging resort community. French Laundry customers have become their friends, and even though they offer free pick-up and delivery along Hwy. 98 and 30A, many customers prefer to come to visit. Ann and J.B. offer dry cleaning services for all types of fabrics, (even leather) and specialize in "resort cleaning" of comforters, rugs, spreads, curtains, and bedding. Shoe repair is even available here. The French Laundry is located at 24 Shannon Ln. at Hwy. 393 just south of Hwy. 98, and is open Monday-Friday 7 am-5:30 pm and Saturday 8 am-1 pm. Call 850-622-0432 or go to www.frenchlaundry@cox.net online.

Index

Cross Reference

Dear Adventurer,

If you are reading this book chances are you are an 'Adventurer.' An 'Adventurer' is a person with a sense of adventure and a curiosity for new and exciting places, people and experiences—both long and short distances. All of the Lady's Day Out books appeal to that sense of adventure and cater to the natural curiosity in all of us.

A Lady's Day Out, Inc., would like to share this gift of the perfect combination between work and travel with our loyal following of readers.

In an effort to expand our coverage area we are looking for adventurous travelers who would like to help us find the greatest places to include in our upcoming editions of A Lady's Day Out. This is a wonderful opportunity to travel and explore some of the best destination cities in the United States.

If you would like more information we would love to hear from you. You may call A Lady's Day Out, Inc. at 1-888-860-ALDO (2536) or e-mail us at www.aladysdayout.com.

Best wishes and keep on exploring, from all of us at A Lady's Day Out, Inc.

"A LADY'S DAY OUT GIVEAWAY"
ENTRY FORM

HAVE FIVE OF THE BUSINESSES FEATURED IN THIS BOOK SIGN YOUR ENTRY FORM AND YOU ARE ELIGIBLE TO WIN ONE OF THE FOLLOWING: WEEKEND-GET-AWAY AT A BED AND BREAKFAST, DINNER GIFT CERTIFICATES, SHOPPING SPREE GIFT CERTIFICATES OR $250 CASH.

1. _____
   (NAME OF BUSINESS)   (SIGNATURE)

2. _____
   (NAME OF BUSINESS)   (SIGNATURE)

3. _____
   (NAME OF BUSINESS)   (SIGNATURE)

4. _____
   (NAME OF BUSINESS)   (SIGNATURE)

5. _____
   (NAME OF BUSINESS)   (SIGNATURE)

NAME: _____

ADDRESS: _____

CITY: _____ STATE: _____ ZIP: _____

PHONE#: _____ E-MAIL: _____

WHERE DID YOU PURCHASE BOOK? _____

OTHER TOWNS OR BUSINESSES YOU FEEL SHOULD BE INCORPORATED IN OUR NEXT BOOK. _____

NO PURCHASE NECESSARY. WINNERS WILL BE DETERMINED BY RANDOM DRAWING FROM ALL COMPLETE ENTRIES RECEIVED. WINNERS WILL BE NOTIFIED BY PHONE AND/OR MAIL.

MAIL TO:
A LADY'S DAY OUT
8563 BOAT CLUB ROAD
FORT WORTH, TX 76179

FAX TO:
817-236-0033
PHONE: 817-236-5250
WEBSITE: www.aladysdayout.com